T0365115

The Big Secret to Unlocking the Power of God's Word… Simply Believe It!

NOLA ESTWICK

WESTBOW°
PRESS
A DIVISION OF THOMAS NELSON
& ZONDERVAN

Except otherwise indicated, all Scripture has been taken
from the King James Version of the Bible.

The quotations from the works of Ellen White are used
with the kind permission of the Ellen White Estate.

The author assumes full responsibility for the accuracy of
the Ellen White quotations cited in this book.

Cowman, Charles E. Streams in the Desert. Grand Rapids,
Michigan: Zondervan Publishing House, 1965, April 4.

Brief quotations taken from Streams in The Desert are used with
the kind permission of Zondervan Publishing House.

WestBow Press books may be ordered through booksellers or by contacting:

WestBow Press
A Division of Thomas Nelson & Zondervan
1663 Liberty Drive
Bloomington, IN 47403
www.westbowpress.com
1 (866) 928-1240

ISBN: 978-1-4908-3628-7 (sc)
ISBN: 978-1-4908-3629-4 (e)

Library of Congress Control Number: 2014908054

Printed in the United States of America.

WestBow Press rev. date: 6/2/2014

Contents

Acknowledgements

——•❂•——

I would like to express profound gratitude to all those who contributed to making this publication a reality. Extra special thanks go to my family: My husband Andy, who acted as my 'technical person.' He was instrumental in formatting the manuscript, doing all the footnotes and giving very helpful tips and being very supportive generally. Andy is a short man, but not short of all the qualities which have made him an excellent husband and a consistently supportive mate for the past thirty one years.

I also express thanks to our three daughters, all of whom have played their individual roles, acting as sounding boards when necessary and being supportive of their crazy mother. Special thanks to Debbie-Ann for her stints of proofreading and her very constructive comments.

Being a very avid reader with a keen eye for writing 'felonies', I employed Donna-Lee as my 'nit-picker'. She did an excellent job at spotting glitches and was able to set her mother straight! Thanks Dons! A big 'thank you' also goes to my youngest daughter, Dereka-Lynn, who is a born encourager.

Despite failing eyesight, my Mum also did her part in proofreading and offering very helpful suggestions. She is like a solid wall behind me. Her encouragement went as far as suggesting that I could even write a devotional. Maybe, I will take her up on it someday.

I am deeply indebted to Miss Dawn Minott for all her 'technical assistance'. At my invitation, her insightful and constructively critical comments, challenged me at times to rethink, revise and rewrite, all for greater clarity and expressive force. Dawn was able to make her contribution from all the way in New York, as we made use of the technology to facilitate her involvement. I am especially grateful to Dawn because, busy as she was with her own publication, she still took the time to render assistance. I wish her resounding success with her new publication: 'Moments – A Heart's Journey'.

I also express profound thanks to Mrs. Phyllis Murrell for her helpfulness and words of commendation. Phyllis, a retired professional secretary, of no mean calibre, and my Mum's lifelong friend, did not hesitate when I asked her for assistance. She is very methodical and meticulous. Her comments and suggestions were well thought out and offered with loving tactfulness. She wrote me a very beautiful letter where she indicated that she thought the book would be of great encouragement to those who try to follow the Christian faith. Phyllis, thank you very much. The early morning impression to call and ask for your assistance was indeed divinely inspired.

Since this publication was a real work in progress, as I kept adding on new insights, I laid hands suddenly on two educators and requested their assistance in a last minute thorough sweeping over of the entire document. Mrs Shirlene Payne, a retired school teacher and a very supportive sister in Christ, did yeoman service. Thank you very much Shirlene for your unstinting help with this manuscript and may I add, also the one with the Prayer Letters.

Special thanks also go to my teaching colleague Mrs. Beverley Walters for accepting to review the manuscript despite a very hectic schedule. Your eagle eye was appreciated. To the perfectionists, if anything was missed, I accept full responsibility.

Thanks are also extended to Miss Anya Stephens for so willingly agreeing to take some photos. Despite her busy schedule as a student pursing her Art degree, she very enthusiastically acceded to my request. We had great fun!

Mrs. Donna Evelyn, my friend and colleague, will be very surprised that she is mentioned here. Donna, it was actually you who dropped the seed in my heart to 'do something' with the Word of God. I showed Donna how I was using my IPOD to interact more with the Word and also told her about my prayer journals where I collated spiritual themes.

I remember well the morning in the staff room when she became very enthused and suggested that others were getting the Word out in different creative ways and I should think about doing it as well. Well, Donna, I did more than think, I acted. The Holy Spirit watered the idea you inspired and so you are holding the result in your hands. Thank you for encouraging in me a creative love for the Word as we have often shared our 'Text for the day'. Thank you too for always being so encouraging.

I heartily thank Dr. Andrew Harewood for his foreword to this publication. Heartfelt thanks are also extended to my endorsers: The Hon Robert. L. Morris, Pastor Randy Skeete, Pastor Terence Haynes, Mr. Vince Yearwood, Dr. Stephen Pilgrim and Professor Pedro Welch for their kind words of recommendation. By God's grace, I believe that the publication will in no way belie the sentiments expressed.

I want to thank all those persons who have 'kept me in prayer'. Some of you I know, like Bro Marc Dabaiya, the eternal optimist, who would facetiously tell me that I will outlive the undertaker. But there are others I do not know, who may have lifted me in prayer, not out of fear for my 'folly' or any impending feeling of calamity, but from a stance of faith. Thank you! Maybe, you will introduce yourself someday.

There are yet others who may not have understood my journey, and unfortunately, may have responded in ways consistent with that lack of understanding. They are certainly forgiven. I pray that this publication makes it evident to all, how God has used His Word in my life to strengthen me on the path He charted for me. "I know the plans I have for you..." (See Jeremiah 29:11.) It is my desire that all of us would find our strength and solace in God *when* our time of testing comes.

Though not directly involved in this publication, I must express thanks and pay tribute to the late Mrs. Ruby St. John, my former English teacher at the Christ Church Girls' Foundation School. She greatly contributed to my life and my writing. She was heavily involved in the main publication which is to follow. Were my mentor and second mother alive today, I know that her joy would know no bounds to see how God has led with this first publication.

I express thanks to all my other friends and well-wishers whose encouragement and kind support over the years have partially contributed to the stamina which has led to this publication. You know exactly who you are! Thank *you* for being in the 'balcony of my life'.

We normally leave the best wine for the last. The final Persons I have to thank would be my 'Dream Team.' Words are totally insufficient to thank the Three Beings who have stood solidly by my side in my life's journey. There is a Prayer Letter in the main publication which is dedicated to the Triune God – God the Father, God the Son, and God the Holy Spirit and the distinct roles each of them has played. Though words are woefully inadequate, I would have to say "Team, I must thank you, not only with words but with my very life for the execution of 'Mission Impossible!'

Dedication

This book is dedicated to my three beautiful and talented daughters: Donna-Lee Hargrett Nee Estwick, Debbie-Ann Estwick and Dereka-Lynn Estwick. They are great young ladies and have all been specially blessed by God as He has promised.

My desire for them all is that they would mature into women of faith who love the Word of God and will search it diligently to discover God's will and purpose for their lives.

I wish for them an exciting spiritual life in God where they can tap into all the spiritual blessings He has in store for them, written in their book of life, even before they became foetuses in my womb.

Dons, Peck, Dex, love you all! You know your mother is a bit crazy but there has always been some measure of method in her madness!

I also dedicate this publication to my dear mother, Pauline Sarjeant, who died on April 20, 2013, in the midst of my working on this publication. My Mum stood like a grand old oak tree against the backdrop of my life and was one hundred percent supportive of all my endeavours. As her one and only child, she loved me dearly.

My mother has left us all a marvellous legacy of faith and trust in God. I was able to prove the validity of the promises of God right in the crucible of her passing. Standing on those wonderful promises of strength found in the Word of God was like standing on the Rock of Gibraltar. Could my Mum be alive to know how God has led, she would have been very proud of an achievement of which she was certainly a great part. I so look forward to seeing her on resurrection morning. She is gone but will never be forgotten!

**Standing from left to right: Donna-Lee, Andy,
Dereka-Lynn and Debbie-Ann.
Sitting: Pauline Sarjeant, my Mum and me, Nola.**

Foreword

—•❈•—

My years in the leadership arena have taught me that a leader is any person who takes up the challenge of a cause and makes it happen. In this publication Nola has sought to creatively capture the versatility and reliability of God's Word, as she has personally experienced it. As a precursor to her main publication in which she has invested seven years of intense writing, this 'mini publication' serves to whet our appetite for the 'main course'.

Nola brings the Word alive by artistically showing how it has been deeply embedded and interwoven in her health journey and spiritual experiences with God. Adopting a conversational style approach, she recaptures with enthusiasm, passion and engaging humor, some aspects of her intriguing saga.

Indeed, the Word of God becomes a vibrant living word only as it burns in our hearts and fuels the drive to live and pursue with passion, God's will and purpose for our lives.

This publication challenges us to go beyond mere mental assent to a depth of belief, which produces not only radical, but *necessary* obedience.

Nola's experiences, and the way she shows how she has applied the Word for her spiritual benefit, demonstrate that there *is* supernatural power in the Word to unlock doors of blessing for ourselves *if we but only believe.*

Andrew R. Harewood, Lieutenant Colonel, Former Deputy Pentagon Chaplain

Endorsements

Nola and I share a friendship that spans more than half of our lives, and from which I have benefited especially from her spiritual and moral guidance, and her undiluted interest in my welfare. What started as a teacher/student relationship became a friendship of peers who shared the avocations of teaching and leadership.

In late 2001, early 2002, I had a valley experience in relation to my health which confirmed the importance of FAITH and TRUST in the Almighty. Nola, her late mom, and their Church, joined in lifting me in their prayers. Nola did even more for me and shared her fabulous letters which were written when she was in the midst of her own valley experience or 'health adventure' as she has captioned her journey.

Nola's first published book which I highly recommend to readers is a testimony to the importance to the preeminent values of TRUST and FAITH. In the Gospels of Matthew and Luke, it is confirmed that those with faith "as a grain of mustard seed", can move a mountain, or pluck up a sycamore tree by its roots, and transplant it in the sea. Proverbs advises that we must trust in the Lord with all our might and not lean on our own understanding.

Nola has distilled the wisdom in these biblical injunctions and her first book is a testimony that she has her mustard seed and more.

As a writer she communicates in an engaging style producing many powerful and deep insights dressed in the cloak of humour. Her glowing acknowledgement of her multiple roles as daughter, wife, mother, and friend illuminates her work, and she is generous in paying tribute to the works, words, and mentors who have influenced her. For those who want to find their own mustard seed, and who wish to experience the richness of love conveyed in the word, this book is highly recommended.

H.E. The Hon Robert. L. Morris, Barbados Ambassador to CARICOM and the Association of Caribbean States(ACS)

******

This work represents a journey into a previously under-explored aspect of our spirituality. Written by an author who has all of the advantages of a special experience, its authenticity is revealed in the willingness to accept the weakness of humanity while acknowledging that the answer to this weakness is full reliance on the Creator's understanding. I expect that this will be a must-read, particularly for those of us who are engaged in our own struggles with a humanity that needs to be taught the lesson of faith.

Pedro L. V. Welch (Professor)
Dean (Faculty of Humanities, University of the West Indies)

***

"It certainly comes right home and speaks to issues that we all face daily. Often witty and humorous, but always reveals the Word in an inspirational and fresh way. A must-read for those who love His name and treasure His Word."

Terence Haynes – B.Sc.; BA; MA (can.)
Health Director – St. Vincent & the Grenadines Mission
RLP SDA Primary School Board Chairman
Ordained District Pastor

******

"If Adam had obeyed God, the world would not be the moral sewer it is today. When God speaks, He desires obedience from the heart. This willing submission to God's word is the golden vein of truth in this inspiring work. For that reason, I recommend it without hesitation. Obedience is life."

Pastor Randy Skeete
International Evangelist

******

"Personal, practical, pulsating and prayer-based, a life-story that will strengthen your faith in God, change your outlook on life and how to deal with the sometimes daunting but 'God-allowed' situations we often face. As you discover the true power of God's Word and the fact that it's still effective today as it was when the Word walked among men healing the sick; you will be challenged, encouraged, changed and better prepared for the rest of your life."

Mr. Vincent Yearwood
Church Elder
Business Leader

******

It gives me great pleasure to endorse this great feat of spiritual and emotional victory captured in almost two hundred pages of beauty, style and poise. Over the past years, as I often visited and communicated regularly with Nola and her household, I couldn't help but observe her tenacity and dogged determination in staying on course with this original 'book project' – as it is often called. And now this publication is added as a precursor to that project!

Nola's commitment to 'share her journey' is beyond admiration. Despite the illness of her mother; the challenges of her career; her own health journey, which is espoused as a *setup* and not a *setback*, she remained steadfast to this goal. I would say: "Well done, Nola! History will reveal that a testimony to this journey would be the many way-marks or milestones along the way that served to punctuate her steps with much-needed rest-stops or filling-stations.

Nola's journey has been nothing short of a deep inspiration to me personally. I want to thank her for taking the time to chronicle it in such poetic and literary style. I am sure that many a weary soul will find comfort and solace in the God who guided her life so carefully and consistently over the years. From a deeply personal perspective, there were times when Nola sent me 'Prayer Letters' which she had penned, and I shared them with my family; because these were some challenging times for us too, in one way or another. It was then that her 'Prayer Letters' of encouragement proved to be rather timely and important enhancers of my own spiritual walk with God, as well as that of my family.

I unreservedly endorse this book as a divinely appointed and written testimony of inspiration, guidance and love. As such, I highly recommend it as a must-read for anyone whose life may seem to take a turn which appears confusing. Or maybe, you are someone who is experiencing some punctuation marks in your journey that may seem uncomfortable. Remember Nola! Remember the God who brought her through! For He can also do it for you!

In closing, you would forgive me for singling out at least one statement, from the many in the publication, which has ministered especially to me. Interestingly, the name reflects my own: "Being a Pilgrim".

Great people are those who, because their pilgrim purpose is to glorify God, can see the potential wrapped up in problems. They ask: "What can I learn from this? What is the Lord seeking to teach me? What does He want me to dare to ask and expect?"

Dr. Stephen Pilgrim, PhD, MCIM, MIMgt
University Vice President (former),
University Lecturer
International Business Consultant

Introduction

———•❀•———

Dear Readers:

This book serves as a precursor to my 'real', as in full, publication. In 2003, I started what I have termed a 'health and faith adventure with God'. The word 'adventure' is by no means a misnomer! The Holy Spirit impressed me to document my journey and to share my experiences. I have done so, not only through writing, but via numerous speaking appointments over the years in Barbados. I have also shared my testimony in Trinidad, Antigua and as far away as the USA.

I coined the term "Prayer Letters", a term which I believe has captured the essence of my writing. The first Prayer Letter, written in September 2003, is captioned, *An Invitation to A Prayer Adventure*. The final letter, Prayer Letter # 61, entitled, *Passing The Baton of Faith*, was completed in August 2010.

It has been *seven* years of very enjoyable, exciting and transparent writing. Many blessings have been embedded in the very act of writing. I have written quite candidly and humorously too, about my various experiences and encounters. In some ways it has been like writing from the very eye of a storm; and, this has been peculiarly thrilling.

In a book I recently acquired, *What Happens When Women Say Yes to God, the* writer, *Lysa Terkeurst*, makes the point that God has already worked out the details of what our obedience will accomplish and it is good. She adds that: "We need not fear what our obedience will cause to happen in our life. We should only fear what our disobedience will cause us to miss."[1]

Words fail to express my joy in being radically obedient to God. How would I ever have known that there would be so much to write about? It was surely a leap of faith! In the first Prayer Letter, dated September 29, 2003, I wrote: "I plan by the grace of God to document this experience and publish it in a book someday... to the honour and glory of an Awesomely Wonderful God! Jehovah Shalom!"

The girth of the letters has so expanded that it really requires time on my part to properly proofread and put on the finishing touches, so that any publisher will snatch up, with glee, this collection of letters, as a work of excellence. Meanwhile, as a precursor to the main publication, I believe this booklet, *The Big Secret of Unlocking The Power of The Word... simply believe it!'* can also serve as a titillating appetizer to the main course. And, in the end, it is my desire that my "life assignment" will be a source of help and encouragement to many.

The purpose of this publication is to show that my intimate engagement of the Word of God has contributed greatly to making my journey one of intrigue and much spiritual excitement. It will be clear how I have applied the promises of God to my experience and how these very promises have functioned as practical, realistic and 'rubber hit the road' solutions to all my needs. I think that the following quotation from the book Education is of monumental importance:

---

[1] Lysa Terkeurst, *What Happens When Women Say Yes to God.* Harvest House Publishers, Eugene, Oregon 97402. (2005) p.45

How to exercise faith should be made very plain.
To every promise of God there are conditions. If we
are willing to do His will, all His strength is ours.
Whatever gift He promises, is in the promise itself.
*"**The seed is the Word of God.**" Luke 8:11. As*
surely as the oak is in the acorn, so surely is the gift
of God in His promise. If we receive the promise,
we have the gift.

Faith that enables us to receive God's gifts is itself
a gift, of which some measure is imparted to every
human being. It grows as exercised in appropriating
the Word of God. In order to strengthen faith, we
must often bring it in contact with the word.[2]

Yes, our faith *must* be brought into contact with the Word. The
Word of God is essentially a dead word to the person who does
not have the faith to believe in its potency. The act of believing,
internalizing and personalizing the Word has resulted in many
practical benefits for me. The Word has served as an excellent
counsellor and encourager. Truly, I have profited beyond measure.
(See Isaiah 48:17)

Inserted on Sunday March 3, 2013

Yesterday, Sabbath March 2, I was invited to be one of the
presenters for the Glen SDA Church Women Ministries Day of
Prayer. When I arrived at Oldbury, the venue for their meeting,
a very spirited session was already underway. The presenter
was speaking about claiming the promises of God and the need
to make the Word of God practical in our experiences. This
generated enthusiastic discussion among the participants about

---

[2]   Ellen G. White, *Education*, (Pacific Press Publishing Association, Mountain
View, California, 1948), p.253

applying the Word to our experiences as we seek to truly believe it and speak it into our lives.

As I sat there, I contained myself, knowing full well I had walked into nothing less than overwhelming and astounding divine corroboration, and affirmation, of what I have attempted to do in this book. All I could say internally, as I quietly absorbed it all, was: "Wow Lord! Wow!" He has *always* been a "wow" God to me.

Hopefully, as these women eventually read this publication, they will become strong witnesses to the fact that, much that was said in the discussion, has dovetailed remarkably with what I have chronicled of my journey with God's word, which I have found to be really fascinating. There always seems to be that perfect text to fit your circumstances. His Word is indeed timeless. I have been rejuvenated and energized by it.

> *I love Lysa Terkeurst's encouragement to us, to see life as an adventure with God, and as such, even the rough patches can be handled with grace. She posits that we can be "...full of adventure and yet not (be) worn out from the journey"*[3].

At the beginning of the Christmas holidays in 2012, when God first impressed upon me the call to chronicle my journey through His word, I never, for a second, imagined that it would have mushroomed to the extent which it has.

There were many times when I said to myself: *"Okay this is it, I dun now,"* only to have many more subsequent "dun now" moments because time and time again something else would hit my consciousness – while in the gym, at the beach, in the shower,

---

[3] Lysa Terkeurst, *What Happens When Women Say Yes to God*, Harvest House Publishers, Eugene, Oregon 97402 (2007) p 145

listening to "The Bible Experience" (a dramatized reading of the Bible) or, as soon as I awake, that artesian well would seem to burst inside of me. And so, I kept adding on and on.

When I determined that I was really through and sent the final draft to my husband, Andy Estwick, for formatting, I said to him: "If I add anything else, *gimme a cuff*".[4] However, being the sweet husband he is and knowing me too, he understood that my "dun" was of a very elastic nature. But obviously I am truly "dun" since you are reading this! Well, there is always a part two!

The entire project has been very engrossing. At times, I skipped going to the gym because I simply could not tear myself away from what I was doing. I thoroughly enjoyed working on this publication and hope you will have commensurate pleasure as you read.

Over the last ten years in particular, the Word has become like a beach strewn, not with pebbles, but with jewels. I have snatched them up eagerly, like a wild and excited child, dashing madly from one jewel to the other, trying to grab them all.

An hour or more is easily eaten up and I have only scratched the surface of the goldmine of God's Word. I can appreciate the thrill Jeremiah felt when he said: *Thy words were found, and I did eat them; and thy word was unto me the joy and rejoicing of mine heart.* Jeremiah 15:16

I love how this writer creatively captures how scripture must become to us. As you know, some folk 'love their bellies'. Lloyd John Oglivie, says: "Scripture is like food: it must be chewed over, swallowed, and digested for its potency to permeate our thinking and reactions."[5]

---

[4] A cuff in this context would be a friendly punch

[5] Lloyd John Oglivie, *Falling Into Greatness*, Thomas Nelson Inc., Nashville, Tennessee (1984) p. 51

God's Word is replete with promises, referred to as 'great and precious' (see 2 Peter 1:4) and once we meet the conditions, we can soar. Indeed, we can *"mount up with wings as eagles"*, (see Isaiah 40:31) knowing that the sky only, is our limit.

Dear reader, I trust that this book truly grips you. At times, you may chuckle heartily at some of the things I say. Beyond the humour however, is the reality of recognizing that God's Word is our only safe guide. My desire is that the Word of God would truly engage your heart.

Ultimately, my aim is to encourage you to personalize the Word of God for your experiences and for your life's journey. Once you have done this, you will be equipped to stride through any of life's storms with your head held high, courageously walking in all the blessings your loving Heavenly Father prepared for you, **even before you were born**.

Nola Estwick, March 26, 2013

Staying in Step

———— ·•❁•· ————

There is a way that seems right unto a man but the end thereof are the ways of death. Proverbs 16:25

The steps of a good man are ordered by the LORD: and he delighteth in his way. Psalm 37:23

As Christians, when we come to a crossroad experience in our life's journey, we do not have to guess or do "Eenymeeny Minnie mo"[6] to decide how to proceed. The Christian has before him the avenue of prayer in seeking God's will on the matter at hand. It was to such a crossroad I came in 2003, when I had to make a decision regarding my health.

Since I was ignorant, I sought God's wisdom. Regrettably, on critical matters, should the wrong course be chosen, one may not know until it is too late. If God orders your steps, then it means you will walk in the centre of His will for you and you need not stumble. God Himself will teach us how to choose. *"Who, then, is the man that fears the LORD? He will instruct him in the way chosen for him."* Psalm 25:12. Yes, God has an individualized strategy for each of us.

---

[6] This s a game played by West Indian children which involves the random selection of someone

1

God revealed to my spirit very clearly that my journey was not simply about physical healing, but about my eternal salvation, as well as the salvation of others. As the Barbadian saying goes, 'There is more in the mortar than the pestle.' There is more in God's mortar, as it were, than merely granting us our desires. He goes deep, to the very issue of our eternal destiny!

****

Hearing and Obeying God's Voice

His mother saith unto the servants, whatsoever he saith unto you, do it. John 2:5

And when he putteth forth his own sheep, he goeth before them, and the sheep follow him: for they know his voice. And a stranger will they not follow, but will flee from him: for they know not the voice of strangers. John 10:4, 5

Obedience is one thing, but radical obedience takes us to another level. What happens when our decision to obey involves a 'risk', even our very life? Mary's advice to the servants is relevant for all time. I have juxtaposed these two texts as there is a significant inferred connection.

Taking the advice Mary gave the servants as a personal mandate raises some issues. *The servants could see and hear Jesus.* He was there in person. We do not have a physical Jesus with us. What if the instruction we receive is as illogical as the one given to the servants? How do we know when God is communicating? We cannot see Him! Can we be deluded, confusing our own internal thinking with God's voice? The possibility of being deluded may scare some folk away from the adventurous path of hearing and obeying the voice of God.

John tells us clearly how to discern God's voice. Be His sheep! If you truly are, you will hear Him speaking. The sheep follow the shepherd *because they know His voice.* Though there are several sheep, He calls each one by name. Because of the intimacy of relationship between each sheep and the shepherd, the sheep does not need to worry about mixing up voices. One of the things God clearly told me to do, was to document my experience. I am very glad that I understood and obeyed that instruction.

Moving away now from the figurative to the literal, and to life itself, we are all sheep and in need of guidance. I can best understand God's voice in the context of an intimate personal relationship with Him. That kind of relationship, which it is our privilege to have, has *absolutely nothing* to do with "holier than thouness", spiritual arrogance or being "up there". The best position from which God's voice is discernible is at the foot of the cross, with your will surrendered to the will of God!

****

Mightier Than the Sword ... is the Pen!

————•❁•————

> *Then the LORD said to Moses, "Write down*
> *these words, for in accordance with these*
> *words I have made a covenant with you and*
> *with Israel." Exodus 34: 27*
>
> *Then the LORD said to Moses, "Write this on*
> *a scroll as something to be remembered and*
> *make sure that Joshua hears it ..." Exodus 17:14*

I love to write... but not just anything. I like to write the things God impresses upon my heart; little gems He drops in my spirit. I love to write out my thoughts to God in response to what I read. I guess that is why I eat up prayer journals very quickly. I wrote to God somewhere in a prayer journal that I had never really done anything for Him. God knows how I love to write letters.

Many years ago I had a prayer letter writing project where I wrote to two individuals over a long period of time. As I prayed for them at that point in their spiritual experiences, I was documenting the movements of God as I saw them. At the end of a specified time, I handed those letters over to the individuals, so they could see for themselves what I had been writing.

Writing those letters was a real spiritual adventure for me, as I tapped into the experiences of those persons. That writing expedition showed me that God certainly very intimately involves

Himself in the affairs of our lives. As it relates to documenting my own adventures, I chuckled to myself as I thought God may have said: 'Well, Nola loves writing so much, let Us give her some of her own experiences to write about. She will have some fun doing so!'

In September 2003, when I started to chronicle my spiritual health adventure, it was indeed with much excitement that I commenced this writing journey.

I naively shared one or two of those first letters with some folk, thinking they would have caught my excitement and be as enthused as I was. Alas! I was deluded. Afterwards, I reflected that some of the deep spiritual themes I am now reading, and thoroughly enjoying, had I read those *same things*, years ago, the impact would definitely not have been the same. For me, it would have been like throwing pearls before swine. What I guess has made the difference is my perception of things. Our understanding of some spiritual material depends not only on the material itself, but more so on our *readiness* which is impacted by various factors. The passage of time can affect one's perception of a situation. So I am quite understanding of those who may not have initially understood and were silent – a pregnant silence, maybe.

However, I did have some very enthusiastic and 'gung ho' readers. Three of them in particular stand out. One is my friend, Joycelyn Payne, who avidly read the letters and gave excellent feedback. She was not silent. She spoke of her enjoyment and even wrote me letters. That encouraged me. I wrote one letter which I called *Women Mentoring Women* where I incorporated Joyce's comments. That letter represents a great teaming up on our part. See the appendix.

Another was Karen Lorde, a former colleague. She devoured the letters even while completing her PHD in England. Amazingly, she was also working on a manuscript at the time. She was awarded the most prestigious Frank Collymore Literary award for two of her publications. In the early days, my friend Mrs. Julie Williams, was also a very avid reader despite her very demanding schedule.

Then, of all persons there was my former English teacher, the late Mrs Ruby St. John. Her comments and feedback, as friend and proof-reader, were heartfelt and invaluable. She was the very epitome of encouragement. What awesome divine orchestration! My very own beloved English teacher! And to think, she was in her eighties, but still bright and sharp as ten buttons!

Spiritual writing has always been my passion. As we say in Bajan, the 'mobaton' of prayer journals I have accumulated over the years tell their own story. One excellent way to remember all the experiences we have with God, all the miracles of answered prayer, is simply *to write them down.*

Writing is also very therapeutic and enables you to stand on the outside of your experience, as it were, and write objectively about it. I believe God knows how short our memories are and so He encourages us in the Word to write down what He tells us. On more than one occasion, as soon as I awoke, a thought has formed in my mind, not merely a thought, but more so a message. Scrambling up, I would hastily write it in my prayer journal.

By consistent writing, I am able to keep, as it were, a dossier of God's interventions in my life, in the 'nitty gritty' affairs of everyday living. By doing this, I am cementing, deep inside of me, that God is not only *very real* but deals with me on an *individual* basis. This serves to build my confidence in Him.

When we have a strong confidence in God, buttressed by 'empirical data', to use statistical jargon, it is so much easier to put our entire trust in Him. This is because we have documented proof; we have our *personal evidence*, which no one can gainsay. We know that God is a Man of His word. We become better and better acquainted with God, not so much by *reading* about Him, but more by having *experiences* with Him.

We encourage faith in others when we write about authentic encounters with God. It is a way of putting a face on Him. Our words have a certain kind of immortality about them. Even when we are gone, the powerful residual effects of our words remain. I enjoy and am richly blessed by many writers who left million dollar legacies in their spiritual writings.

Writing also allows others into an experience they would otherwise have never known about, had we not written. It serves to bring clarity, as well, to those who, looking over the paling of our life, saw no stars, only brown grass...

Personal spiritual writing should never be seen as an academic exercise. Your entries in your spiritual journal can be solely for your own enjoyment. I recollect some years ago a message that I shared at the Chance Hall SDA church. At the end of the service, I was met at the door by a sweet old lady. She was in her eighties at the time. With tears in her eyes, she held my hands and said with obvious regret: 'I have had many experiences with God, *but I never had the sense to write them down.*' What if she had? For her children and grandchildren, she may have opened a window to the engaging character of God and His intimate dealing with us, His children... if only she had documented her experiences.

Keeping a prayer journal is not an academic chore, far from. It's a way of talking to God and might just be the genesis of a wonderful creative project. Happy writing!

The Dilemma of Choice - Not to Choose *is to Choose...*

---- ⚙ ----

Who is he that condemneth? It is Christ that died, yea rather, that is risen again, who is even at the right hand of God, who also maketh intercession for us. Romans 8:34

Some decisions are easier than others and we are unable to determine the repercussions of what we do, or don't do, as we do not have what God possesses, which is foresight. The details surrounding my decision are outlined in the main publication, as well as in an article in the Nation Newspaper Better Health issue December 2011. But to succinctly say, I had to decide whether to proceed with a hysterectomy which was recommended, as one medical practitioner indicated, as he thought, that I was losing weight as a result of fibroids. I casually decided that I would go ahead with the procedure. I did not specifically pray about my decision as I accepted what was said as being quite logical. I no longer needed my uterus really.

But then a friend, Miss Irisdene Samuel, whom I had not seen in over twenty years, came to Barbados and, as providentially arranged, ended up staying at my home. I apprised her of my plan and she said, as we sat chatting in the children's bedroom in July 2003: 'God wants to heal you, He wants to give you a powerful testimony." I did ponder 'Heal me! There is nothing about fibroids to heal as such. Hmm!'

9

But my friend's comment forced me to see that I had a choice. You know, sometimes it is so much easier to let folk make decisions for you. It takes the pressure off you. If something goes awry, you can always blame the person who advised you. So, it was a crossroad situation in the sense that I had to decide whether to change course, or proceed with my original intention. I really did not know what to do. I prayed – not any casual, light, flippant prayer. I believe that God responded as He saw the sincerity of my heart, and my desire to know what was His will on this seemingly simple health matter.

A very clear response came in my devotional reading (Streams in The Desert, July 20) a day or two after my focus shifted, as I have documented in Prayer Letter #1. Part of the response went thus:

> *He has gone in for you into the inner chamber, and already holds up your name upon the palms of His hands; and the messenger which is to bring you your blessing, is now on his way, and the Spirit is only waiting your trust to whisper in your heart the echo of the answer from the throne, "It is done."* [7]

The remainder of the quotation goes on to make the point that God corrects the errors in our prayers and then presents them as His own request on our behalf. A major part of the life of prayer is our ability to understand what God is saying when He responds. This is a very personal matter. If you doubt that He will respond, then it is a waste of time praying. *In that statement, I knew that God was speaking directly to me.* Hence, the idea that *it is done while it is being done* has characterised my journey.

1 John 5:14&15 indicate that the assurance we can have in God is that if we have asked according to His will, and have the

---

[7]   Streams in The Desert July 20

10

confidence that He has heard us, then we can be assured that we have, or have been granted our request. The paradox of faith, which many will not understand, is that it is possible to have what you do not actually see. Things assured in the spiritual realm may not be immediately manifested in the physical realm. That is the essence then of *'faith is the substance of things hoped for, the evidence of things not seen.'* Things which are supernatural brook logical explanations!

Some years after reading that Rhema word from 'Streams', I was delighted to find a strong confirmatory comment in the book *The Desire of Ages*. This book happens to be one of my favourite life changing books. What an uncanny repetition of what I had read in July 2003. The writer, Ellen White says:

> *He (Jesus) explained that the secret of their (the disciples) success would be in asking for strength and grace in His name. He would be present before the Father to make request for them. The prayer of the humble suppliant He presents as His own desire in that soul's behalf. Every sincere prayer is heard in Heaven. It may not be fluently expressed; but if the heart is in it, it will ascend to the sanctuary where Jesus ministers and He will present it to the Father without one awkward stammering word, beautiful and fragrant with the incense of His own perfection.*[8]

Once God says something is done, then no matter how 'undone', it may look to our eyes, we have to believe what God has said. Abraham had to do it. If we truly *believe* that Jesus is indeed our Intercessor and our hearts are not being deceitful in any way as we approach our Heavenly Father in prayer, there needs

---

[8]   Ellen G. White, *The Desire of Ages*, Pacific Press Publishing Association, 1350 Villa Street, Mountain View, California 94042, (1898) p 67

be no panic in our experience when we have to make decisions. The words of the prayer need not be perfect. The prayer may be faulty in some way but Jesus looks at the heart. So praying could *never* be about prettily crafted impressive sounding words.... it is always about the heart.

****

Are you a 'Prayer Warrior'?

—————————•◦❋◦•—————————

For the weapons of our warfare are not carnal,
but mighty through God to the pulling down of
strongholds. 2 Corinthians 10:4

You may have responded negatively to the question posed. Possibly, it's because you see being a 'prayer warrior' as some exclusive, elitist kind of activity which is for reserved for the spiritually superior who have some extra special scoop on God.

Ron Halvorsen in his book *Prayer Warriors* intimates that once you enter the Christian army, you automatically are called to be a prayer warrior. Regrettably, this term has fallen into disrepute. In some quarters, the feeling which has emerged is that the word 'warrior' has parted ways with 'prayer'. As a result, the term has been associated with being contentious, quarrelsome, bossy, argumentative and aggressive. What a pity that such negative connotations are associated with a very wholesome activity. Someone suggested maybe 'Prayer Agent' could be substituted. What's in a name? Sometimes, it could be quite a lot.

A true prayer warrior, one at heart, should be the most loving, peaceful, affable and easy to get along with person. The weapons of warfare are not used *against* others but *for* their benefit. I have always felt that we should never convey to others that *only some* people have power in praying, *only some* people have access to God, *only some* people can 'get their prayers answered'.

13

Granted, some individuals, *called by God*, espouse prayer as a ministry and may be doing an excellent job as they sacrifice time for the benefit of others. However, each of us must eventually come to know how to pray for ourselves, how to tap into the heart of God and know what He wants us to do. God tells us to come to Him when we are burdened. He will give us rest. (See Matthew 11:28) He did not tell us to run to our friend first. One spiritual writer says that we must run to *the throne and not the phone.*

Our dependence must *always* be on God, *not on people: the Pastor, the elder, or the best friend.* They may play a part in encouragement, but good as they may be, some friends will backpedal on you. Sometimes in their time of need, individuals run to others before they seek God, those 'others' do not have anything inside of them to give. *You can never give what you do not possess.* But God's resources are infinite. He *always* has to give. He is *never* too busy and He will *never* backpedal. He will give you the correct advice as He is the One who wrote your life plan.

The following quotation is absolutely correct: *"The promises of God are full and abundant and there is no need for anyone to depend on humanity for strength. To all that call upon Him, God is near to help and succor."*[9]

So, you *are* a prayer warrior, not a 'surwarrior'![10]

Confidently take up your weapons: the Word of God and prayer and go fight your battles, the correct ones, *in the strength of the Lord*!!

****

[9] Ellen G. White. TM, p. 381

[10] A 'surwarrior is a Bajan/West Indian expression for a quarrelsome and contentious person who is given to conflict

Act As If...Until It Is...

———————•❁•———————

This is the confidence that we have in our relationship with God: If we ask for anything in agreement with his will, he listens to us. If we know that He listens to whatever we ask, we know that we have received what we asked from Him. 1 John 5:14 &15 CEB (Common English Bible)

Prayer is a lifestyle. We may all have passed through the infantile stage of thinking that the essence of prayer was simply begging God for things. We loved that proverbial corpulent Santa God who dispensed goodies from the heavily laden bag slung over His shoulder. Ho! Ho! Ho!

But as we grew in our walk with God, we came to realize that prayer is more than a 'gimme gimme' approach. It is not simply about God dishing out things to us as we send in our 'wish list'. Real true genuine prayer is about a lifestyle of communion with God and not merely a sporadic activity we engage in when we run into trouble and desire immediate extrication.

If truth be spoken, there are some folk who have absolutely nothing to do with God... until their health begins to fail. Then in panic they beat a hasty retreat to the Great Physician for instantaneous healing. Those who use prayer primarily as a 'quick fix' for their problems may be totally oblivious of the laws and principles which govern prayer as a *science*. Very poignant is this comment from the book Education:

> *"Prayer and faith are closely allied. In the prayer of faith, there is a divine science; it is a science that everyone **who would make his life work a success must understand**."* (My emphasis)[11]

I was reminded of the deep nature of prayer, and the principles involved, as I pondered this writer's insightful exposition:

> *When prayer defines what we are to do and what the Lord will provide to make it possible, we must act as if the blessing has been realised. We can thank the Lord in advance that what He gave us the courage to envision, the boldness to ask for, and the confidence to expect, will be done by Him in His way and in His timing. We ask once and thank Him thousands of times as we wait for the fulfillment of the vision He has given. Often our trust must be expressed in a step of faith that makes us participants with the Lord in the unfolding of His will.*[12]

I read the above quotation in February 2013 but many years earlier, I was tutored again by the divinely inspired prolific writer Ellen White when she said in the book Education:

> *We need look for no outward evidence of the blessing. The gift is in the promise, and we may go about our work assured that what God has promised He is*

---

[11] Ellen G. White, *Education*, Pacific Press Publishing Association, Mountain View, CA (1903) p 257

[12] Lloyd John Oglivie, *Falling Into Greatness*, Thomas Nelson Inc., Nashville, Tennessee (1984) p. 185

> *able to perform, and that the gift, which we already*
> *possess, will be realized when we need it most. To*
> *live thus by the Word of God means the surrender*
> *to Him of the whole life.*[13]

It would be great idea to read that entire chapter entitled *Faith and Prayer.* Her exposition and counselling are par excellent. Paste the following site in your browser window and you will immediately hit the jackpot: http://www.ellenwhite.info/books/bk-ed-30.htm

You will notice that both writers make the same basic point, but in different words. They both highlight some critical principles in the life of prayer and faith. Because these principles are not understood by many of us, genuine faith is often ridiculed and denigrated by those who *must see to believe*, having failed, ironically enough, to 'see' or understand the principles undergirding the life of prayer and faith.

Oglivie talks of 'thanking the Lord in advance' and 'acting as if the promise has been realized'. Ellen White speaks of going about our work with the assurance that God is able to perform what He has promised and that we are in possession of the gift already.

We can infer similar principles from the comments of both writers. The issue of timing is one. God has a set time, *when we need it most.* Another principle to be inferred is that, once we have prayed, and we are talking about a prayer *led and inspired by the Holy Spirit,* then we must behave as if we have the 'thing' already.

That is certainly crazy and illogical in the natural realm but not so in the spiritual realm. The skeptics will never understand this

---

[13] Ellen G. White, *Education*, Pacific Press Publishing Association, Mountain View, CA (1903) p. 258

and so they will arm themselves with stones for the attack. 'Act as if...' utter madness! Preposterous! The Word on which the bona fide Christian stands says:

> *"And this is the confidence that we have in him, that, if we ask any thing according to his will, he heareth us: And if we know that he hear us, whatsoever we ask, we know that we have the petitions that we desired of him." 1 John 5:14 & 15 KJV*

The choice is always ours. We can act as if we are filled with doubt or filled with faith.... and so it will be unto us! Choose the road... less travelled!

****

Dreaming Prayers and God's Will

———————•◉•———————

The Lord will complete what his purpose is for me. Lord, your gracious love is eternal; do not abandon your personal work in me.
Psalm 138:8 International Standard Version

Nothing stimulates, revitalises, energises, or titillates the Christian life, like treating prayer the way it ought to be treated, or seeing it the way it ought to be seen. For some folk, prayer is a boring, obligatory exercise to be hurried through. However, when it is seen as an exciting, dynamic, creative and adventurous way to discover how to tap into the resources of God and to live out the purposes He has determined for our lives, we move to another realm altogether...the realm of the supernatural... the realm of miracles... and adventure!

Let me admit here that I started this new insert on June 8, 2013. I was sure that I was 'dun', (finished), adding no more new stuff, but lo and behold I had to backtrack. A book recently came into my possession, *The Circle Maker*, lent to me by my good buddy, Mrs. Julie Williams. This book, by writer Mark Batterson, set off light bulbs in my head.

As I read yet another creative way to rescue prayer from the doldrums where some have imprisoned it, I kept thinking that 'a rose by any other name is still a rose'. The writer ushers us into another exciting pathway of conceptualising prayer, not for our own purposes, but for the purposes of God.

With respect to the purpose of his book Batterson says:

> *The Circle Maker will show you how to claim God given promises, pursue God sized dreams, and seized God ordained opportunities. You'll learn how to draw circles around your family, your job, your problems, and your goals... Drawing prayer circles is not some magic trick to get what you want from God. God is not a genie in a bottle, and your wish is not His command. His command better be your wish. If it's not, you won't be drawing prayer circles, you'll end up walking in circles.[14]*

This concept stretches my mind to see that my dear mother, now deceased, drew prayer circles around me. This she unknowingly did when she asked God to bless me. I discovered my Mum's Purpose Driven Life Prayer Journal and read some of what she wrote to God as she contemplated His purpose for her and my very existence. It overwhelmed me to tears and 'blew me away'.

I have been drawing prayer circles for years, though not calling it that. Indeed, a rose by any other name is still a rose. I am very glad to see that the writer sets this concept upon a very firm foundation, simply because folk can take prayer concepts and twist them to suit their own purposes. He postulates:

> *Drawing prayer circle starts with discerning what God wants, what God wills. And until His Sovereign will becomes your sanctified wish, your prayer life will be unplugged from its power supply...*

---

[14] Mark Batterson, *The Circle Maker*, Zondervan Publishers, Grand Rapids, Michigan 49530. (2011) p 14

> *getting you what you want isn't the goal; the goal*
> *is glorifying God by drawing prayer circles around*
> *the promises, miracles, and dreams He wants for*
> *you.*[15]

Before I move to the level of application, let me share what Mark
Batterson advocates:

> *Don't just read the Bible. Start circling the promises.*
> *Don't just make a wish. Write down a list of God-*
> *glorifying life goals. Don't just pray. Keep a prayer*
> *journal. Define your dream. Claim your promise.*
> *Spell your miracle*[16].

Journaling has been a part of my life for many years. Reviewing
journal entries from yesteryear is a treat for me at times, as I am
led to recall prayers answered that lay buried under the dusty
cobwebs of the brain, only to be retrieved, because *they were
recorded*. There is much to be said for keeping a record of the
Lord's dealing with us!! (See Habakkuk 2:2)

I was shocked to happen upon an old weather beaten journal
where I had, maybe quite casually, written some desires.. It was
in March 1996. I wrote :

'My Dreams... to write a book... a book of poetry and.... *a
collection of my prayer experiences.*'

A friend who saw the page with my notes and is aware of my
first in 'utero' publication which is in essence a collection of
prayer experiences was amazed and told me that I should take
a picture of the page. I was open-mouthed at what I had written
and the subsequent, what I would have to call, concatenation

---

[15] Ibid. p. 14

[16] Ibid. p. 24

of events. It really seems incredible that the desire which I expressed as a wish, providential orchestration, is in the process of bringing about.

Yes, we can claim Biblical promises, in a bona fide manner, remaining securely in the realm of faith, and not flirting on the peripheries of presumption. The Bible does warn those who grab up God's Word, His covenant and seek to arrogantly wield that Word, while they are resolutely disobedient to His commands. Psalm 50:15 and 16 God speaks:

> *But unto the wicked God saith, What hast thou to do to declare my statutes, or that thou shouldest take my covenant in thy mouth? Seeing thou hatest instruction, and castest my words behind thee. Psalm 50: 16 & 17*

God's Word Translation puts it even clearer: *"But God says to wicked people, how dare you quote my decree and mouth my promises! You hate discipline. You toss my words behind you."*

We who are Christians dare not fall prey to casting God's Word behind us while ostentatiously giving the impression that we believe it. Such spiritually schizophrenic behavior needs to be addressed by the Great Physician. Thank God He is still in the healing business and the healing can lie in simply *believing the Word of God.* (See Psalm 103: 2 & 3)

Blessed In the Land of Famine

---•❀•---

Then Isaac sowed in that land, and received in the same year an hundredfold: and the Lord blessed him. Genesis 26:12

Behold, the eye of the Lord is upon them that fear him, upon them that hope in his mercy; to deliver their soul from death, and to keep them alive in famine. Psalm 33:18

The Lord knoweth the days of the upright: and their inheritance shall be forever. They shall not be ashamed in the evil time: and in the days of famine they shall be satisfied. Psalms 37:18 & 19

As a teacher of English Literature and Language for the past thirty four years, I enjoy bringing my literary analysis skills to assist in ferreting out the deeper meanings of the Biblical imagery, as it relates to the issue of life's vicissitudes. Exploring the implications and applications of the symbolism is quite fascinating.

The Bible addresses the arena of tests and trials under a variety of images: water, fire, valleys, rivers, floods, storms, deserts and famines. The above texts relate to the imagery of the famine. What does that have to do with me as I apply it to my life and circumstances?

In 2003, was the start of a journey of faith and trust in God, but was also a time which could be metaphorised as a time of famine. God told me that the landscape of my life would change. Speaking to me in my reading, He used the initial image of a storm ravaging a landscape to alert me of the coming change.

As the years have passed, I have delved into the Word of God exploring the various images which have engaged my interest and personal application. The metaphor of the famine speaks to a time of change, the landscape is different. During a literal famine, there is a scarcity of water and the vegetation usually dries up, among the other changes in the environment. Parched trees are not expected to produce fruit.

Moving from the literal to the spiritual figurative, opens up to us a breath-taking panoramic view of what God can do for us even in a 'famine' – a time of trial. It is in such a time that those in their land of plenty expect to see those in the land of famine starve to death.

However, God clearly says what He will do and what will happen. The texts identify those who would receive divine favour in the time of famine: the 'upright' and 'those who fear God'. These two qualifying elements, I consider to be inclusive and not exclusive.

Such persons, the texts indicate, shall not be ashamed in the evil time, in the days of famine they shall be satisfied. God would keep them alive and deliver their soul from death. In other words, God would rain blessings on those who love and seek to please Him and honour Him in their famine time.

I want to connect those two texts from the Psalms to what the Bible says of Isaac in his time of literal famine. Read Genesis chapter 26 for the full narrative. There was a famine in the land and God gave Isaac an unusual instruction. He told him in essence to stay put, not to move. (See Genesis 26:2 & 3) Others would logically have moved seeking a place of plenty. Isaac was instructed otherwise. It would have seemed like a risk to remain... even foolish, but He obeyed. The result of his obedience is spelt out in Genesis 26: 12-14.

Isaac planted crops in that land and the same year (*the year of the famine*) reaped a hundredfold, because the LORD blessed him. The man became rich, and his wealth continued to grow until he became very wealthy. He had so many flocks and herds and servants that the Philistines envied him.

Obeying God is always critical. He speaks to us personally. If we are afraid to be different or we must do whatever 'John Q. Public' does, then we will limit ourselves and what we can achieve in God. *Nothing* equals the blessing of God. Not even your worst enemy can deflect it. Balaam discovered this. He simply could not curse where God had given His blessing. Read that very intriguing story in Numbers Chapter 22.

Following the directions of God, I experienced the blessings of God in the time of 'famine' in abundance, indeed a hundredfold.

Three critical points of application are noteworthy: Firstly, what is important for us to understand is that God blesses us *where He has positioned us, not where we have presumptuously placed ourselves.* Secondly, God leads us *individually* and not as a pack. God may direct us not to 'go down to Egypt' as He did with Isaac because He has blessings prepared for us right in the land of the famine. Finally, radical obedience to an instruction from God may seem risky but God does not operate on the basis of trial and error. He is infallible and will direct us aright in every situation.

God's very presence can turn the land of famine into a land of prosperity! A million hats off to a magnificent God!

****

Great And Precious Promises

---·❋·---

Whereby are given unto us exceeding great and precious promises: that by these ye might be partakers of the divine nature, having escaped the corruption that is in the world through lust. 2 Peter 1:4

Claiming the promises of God requires courage and confidence. It's not a 'name it and claim it' kind of game. To take that approach is to trivialize a very serious matter. Conditions are attached to the promises and to claim them while ignoring the conditions would be presumption.

For example, as it relates to health, the apostle John gives us a message from God when he says he wishes that we would prosper and be in health even as our soul prospers. (See 3 John 1:2) Many people want to claim good health, either for their health to be preserved or to be restored. However, they may not see obeying the laws of health and the laws of their being as part of that "claiming process". Is it not then the very height of irony, for critics to sneeringly or suspiciously regard those who have sensibly made lifestyle changes, while the critics themselves wantonly break the laws of health and expect to be preserved in *good health*? There is a Bajan saying "Wuh en catch yah en pass yah"! (This expression means that what has not happened to you as yet, can still occur. The inference is that you should not be arrogantly complacent).

Yes, there are wonderful promises in the Word of God for us. In all areas, not only in the realm of health, is meeting the conditions applicable. But it is still more than meeting the conditions. Behind the promise is the Promiser. If we have any hidden doubts about the Promiser's integrity, and indeed His power to make good His word, we will have difficulty in believing His promises.

The Promiser is a God of both love and power. If He were only a God of love, then He would be impotent and His promises would be equal to a bag of wind. If He were a God of power, without having a heart of love, we would be dealing with a God who could well be tyrannical. Thankfully, there is no dichotomy between God's love and His power. To be reminded of how loving God is, read Psalm 86:15. For a stunning display of His power, no doubt modestly outlined by God Himself, review Job 38. If that leaves you in doubt, then you will always be in doubt!

I love these comments about the promises of God from the 'pen of inspiration':

> *We should take the promises of God, one by one and examine them closely on every side – take in their richness, and be soothed and comforted, encouraged and strengthened by them. God has provided for all the comforts the soul needs.*[17]

> *The promises of God are full and abundant and there is no need for anyone to depend on humanity for strength. To all that call upon him God is near to help and succor.*

> *We are not to believe because we see or feel that God heard us. We are to trust to the promise of God. We*

---

[17] Ellen G. White, *That I May Know Him*, Review and Herald Publishing Association, Washington, D.C (1964) p 213

*are to go about our business believing that God will
do just as He has said He would do, and that the
blessings we have prayed for will come to us when
we need them most.*[18]

*Heaven is full of blessings and it is our privilege to claim the rich
promises of God for our individual selves. We need to seek the Lord
day and night that we may know just what steps to take and just
what we ought to do.*[19]

God's promises are adaptable to all of our needs. I have made
that personal discovery. Contained in this publication is a mere
sample of some of these precious promises and their application
to my life's journey. There are many others I would love to talk
about, but alas I would never be finished, and so I must curtail
myself... or prepare another book.

In 2004 I wrote this poem which is included in Prayer Letter #
8 "Miracles and 'Miracalettes'":

'She is Coming Our Way!!'
Written June 2004

Under Heaven's tree
Lay the mysterious gift, prettily wrapped
Affixed on its surface in letters of gold – my name!
Only waiting, by faith, to be claimed.
"She's not envisaged such a stupendous gift",
I hear the Heavenly Team say.
"Can we get her to look Our way?
There is no time for delay
But, but, would she dare?

---

[18] Ibid p 230
[19] Ellen G. White, *My Life Today*, Review and Herald Publishing Association,
Hagerstown, MD (1952) p 62

Or, would she be consumed with fear?
She has asked for moderate things before
But an insatiable desire burns in her for more.
"I'll inject the thought in her mind.
Indeed, her highest joy she will surely find,"
I hear the Heavenly Comforter say,
"if only she changes course and comes Our way."
And so, one morning as I knelt to pray
Mentally thumbing under which doctor's hand I would lay
Which one I would pull my pocket to pay.....
A voice seemed to say, 'Just stay!'
Distinctly, I heard the whisper in my heart
"Bring it to us
We will fix it right from the start."
Without hesitation and without doubt
No demon in hell, my faith could rout.
My soul reached up, and in faith, that gift was grasped
In my heart, it remains securely clasped.
"Yes!" I hear a triumphant shout.
"She has changed course!
She has turned right about
She is coming our way
All of her fears we will allay
She knows where her power source lies
She will hold on even if it looks as if she will die
But her daring choice will be the catalyst
For joys beyond compare
Her faith will open to her
The vault of Heaven, with its jewels so rare
Reserved only for those who will dare
To step out into space...
Without doubt and WITHOUT FEAR!!
The End

I love this poem which I have shared in several places over the years. We must experientially become acquainted with the

Promiser and truly love the One who condescended to take on our human flesh, Jesus Christ Himself! We can only confidently claim the promises if we have truly seen the heart of the Promiser. He showed His heart at Calvary. For all the promises of God in Him *are* Yes, and in Him Amen, to the glory of God through us. 2 Corinthians 1:20

****

Condition Met... the Promise is Unequivocal!

--- ⚙ ---

Trust in the LORD, and do good; so shalt thou dwell in the land, and verily thou shalt be fed. Delight thyself also in the LORD; and he shall give thee the desires of thine heart. Commit thy way unto the LORD; trust also in him; and he shall bring it to pass. And he shall bring forth thy righteousness as the light, and thy judgment as the noonday. Rest in the LORD, and wait patiently for him: fret not thyself because of him who prospereth in his way, because of the man who bringeth wicked devices to pass Psalm 37: 3 - 7

Let us consider how we can claim God's promises in a practical way. Read all of Psalm 37 in various versions so you grasp firmly what the verses are saying. But for the purposes of our focus now, pay special attention to the first seven verses. As I have read and internalised these verses, I am further cemented in the unassailable truth that God does not lie; He is not an 'equivocator'. It is left to *us* to trust in the integrity of His character.

The promises found in Psalm 37:3-7 are very attractive indeed. Who would not want to take them up and run with them? As I have personalized these promises, they tell me that I would dwell in the land and be fed, God would give me the desires of my heart; He would bring my way to pass, and would make my 'righteousness' to shine like the dawn. He would also vindicate the justice of my cause. Of course, I certainly have no righteousness of my own to shine, except it is mercifully imputed to me, an undeserving sinner.

Each facet of these promises is packed with deep spiritual meaning and deserves further exploration ...which I will leave you to do. Though these weighty promises are up for grabs, as it were, before we can snatch them up and dart away in gleeful delight, we must pause and ponder the conditions. These conditions are spelt out in at least five main words, all action verbs. They indicate what we must do to access the promises. The words are: trust, delight, commit, rest and wait.

Each word denotes a specific action which we are to live out in a practical way in our day to day experience. Take for example the word commit. Many folk commit something to God but then promptly snatch it back from Him, by the time they rise from their knees. But what about if you have truly committed a matter to God, but things appear to be going awry, to your carnal vision? I like the advice of this spiritual writer:

> *"However extraordinary and unexpected may seem to be His guidance, however near the precipice He may take you, you are not to snatch the guiding reins out of His hands."*[20]

The ultimate then of committing something to God is that we have to be able to say, 'Though He slay me, yet I will trust Him.'

We must each experience for ourselves what it means to trust God in the very depths of our being. This can never be a vicarious experience. Our trust must not be in what *we tell God* we want

---

[20] Streams In The Desert, November 21

but in what *He tells us He will give us and do for us*, and on this we need to be certain.

I appreciate the spiritual insight of this writer:

> *God is to be trusted for what He is and not for what He is not. We may confidently expect Him to act according to His nature, but never contrary to it. To dream that God will do this and that because we wish that He would is not faith but fanaticism. Faith can only stand upon truth.*[21]

I believe that God will honour genuine faith – a faith which will rest itself comfortably on the sure promises of His Word. Any radical trusting of God may be interpreted as fanaticism, but God does not back such. When fanaticism goes out on her own limb, she will have to fend for herself.

With faith it will be different. God will have her back. She will not have to lie down in sorrow, stumbling along her pathway and becoming all stressed out and jaded. The writer further states:

> *We may be sure that God will so act as to honour His own justice, mercy, wisdom, power - in a word so as to be himself. Beyond all doubt He will fulfil His promises; and when faith grasps a promise she is on sure ground. To believe that God will give us what He has never promised to give us is mere dreaming. Faith without a promise revealed or implied is folly.*[22]

---

[21] Mrs. Charles E. Cowman, Springs In The Valley, Zondervan Publishing House, grand Rapids, Michigan 49530. (1997) September 21

[22] Ibid, p***

God will not uphold folly and presumption. God will stand back of His promises, not our misguided and unsanctified desires. He made some promises to me, some were very direct. Others I would have inferred, as directed by His spirit in my spiritual reading, both of the Bible and other sound reputable spiritual literature.

I have learnt some significant spiritual truths about the 'fear of the Lord' from Derek Prince's exegesis of this subject. It is clearly revealed that when certain conditions are met, we put ourselves in a favourable position to have the promises fulfilled in our lives. The Word of God very clearly outlines the pathway of those who possess the fear of the Lord. Derek Prince intimates that a submissive attitude toward God is an expression of the fear of the Lord in our lives. His excellent exposition on *The Fear of The Lord* may be accessed at his website.

Submission to the will of God is what opens the doors to His blessings. We cannot have our cake and eat it too, i.e. follow *our own way and plan* and yet expect God to bless us and favour us. Two of the wonderful promises resulting from submissiveness to God's will are found in Proverbs 10:27 which says that the fear of the Lord *prolongs life*, which in essence means that you will live longer with the fear of the Lord, than you would without it. The promise relates to longevity, *not immortality.*

Psalm 25:14 also highlights another significant promise. Here the Word assures us that, 'The secret of the LORD is with those who fear Him, and He will show them His covenant.' My Rhema word given in April 2003 found in Jeremiah 32: 40 & 41 is where God covenanted with me to do me good. In those verses He said He would *delight* to do me good and would plant me in the land...

Because I have never doubted the truth of what God revealed to my heart, it has given me tremendous strength which has allowed me to walk with confidence in God. It has kept me very firm and steady in the midst of the gossip, criticism and negativity that may have swirled around me. None of it had the power to affect my spirit. Faith must have backbone. I can testify to the truthfulness of Proverbs 14:26 and Proverbs 19:23.

If we but truly *take God at His word*, as we so happily *sing*, I am sure God would be thrilled to be given the opportunity to show that He has not suffered any amputations and that though He is the Master of the winds, He does not blow hot air!

****

A Hidden Treasure

Thy word have I hid in mine heart, that I might not sin against thee. Psalm 119:11

I keep your word close in my heart, so that I won't sin against you. CEB

Years ago I started collating what I have called "Journey Texts". I had loads of them printed on cards and I would review them very often. But then I started to give those cards to persons I would visit in the hospital. I have a few left now. In my prayer journal I also have pages and pages of many beautiful texts arranged under my own designated themes: Strength in God, God's timing, guidance, God's faithfulness etc.

Part of my devotion time was spent in reading and learning these texts. I developed my own mnemonic device for memorizing my 'power texts'. I would make a sentence out of texts I wanted to learn by heart, as well as remember their source. This was and still is great fun for me.

For example, one of my memory sentences is: Once you are *acquainted* with Him, you have to *abound* and soar *above*, always walking in *grace*. Each italicized word represents a text which I have memorized and I know exactly where it is found in the Bible. The word *acquaint* triggers Job 22:21 in my mind which says: 'Acquaint now thyself with him and be at peace'. The word *abound* brings to mind 2 Corinthians 9:8 immediately. This text says: And God is able to make all grace abound toward you...' I will leave you to connect the other italicised words to an appropriate text.

Thankfully, God showed me a better and faster way to record texts, rather than writing them all out in my prayer journal as I had been meticulously doing. Utilizing the technology, having been blessed with one of the best gifts I have ever received, I am in the process of transferring all that information to my IPod by simply copying and pasting from my Bible to my notes section. Thank you again, Andy!

With my IPod, I can now interface with God's Word very quickly and in almost any place I happen to be. I can have the Word of God with me now as I walk along the beach, savouring the richness of the promises. I have the *Bible Experience* on my IPod as well. This is a par excellent dramatized reading of the Bible. I can listen while I am doing my exercises in the gym, washing dishes at the sink, hanging out clothes in my backyard. Faith comes by hearing too. Truly, truly, *I am in my element.*

There is tremendous benefit to hiding God's Word in your heart. Reading it is great but having it inside of you, written in your heart is even better. God says that He would write His law in our hearts. Once that Word becomes embedded in your heart, it makes it more difficult to fall into sin. Unbelief is a sin. We may not conceptualize it as such. Jerry Bridges categorises it in his book, 'Respectable Sins', as one of our...yes... 'respectable sins'. Unbelief is insidious in its nature because it strikes at the very nature and character of God. When we doubt His Word we are certainly calling into question His integrity. Each of us must individually prove for ourselves that God is our faithful and loving Heavenly Father. He can be no less. (See Matthew 7:11)

Take some time and search out the promises in the Bible which can enrich your life. Read the Word. Listen to the Word. Learn the promises. Don't stay at the knowledge level. Take a quantum leap - move to application. You will be richly blessed!

****

Good Ground

---·•❋•·---

But he that received seed into the good ground is he that heareth the word, and understandeth it; which also beareth fruit, and bringeth forth, some an hundredfold, some sixty, some thirty. Matthew 13:23

The seed cast on good earth is the person who hears and takes in the News, and then produces a harvest beyond his wildest dreams. The Message Bible

'Just believe…'The title of this publication which ends with the words 'simply believe it' is not intended to trivialize the matter of taking God at His word. It is easy to believe and it is hard to believe. Yes, a paradox!

Simply believing is not as simplistic as it may seem. The soil of the heart is a critical factor in determining whether God's Word, like a seed, will take root and flourish. Explaining the meaning behind the symbolism in the Parable of the Sower, Jesus explains the various types of heart soil into which the Word is sown.

It is Satan's aim that the Word of God does not take root and flourish. However that may be achieved is inconsequential. In fact he may sardonically say: 'Let them read the Word, let them argue over, as to who is right and who is wrong, but *never let them believe it*!" The ideal heart soil is found in the person who hears the Word and incorporates it into his life style, with *visible* effect.

But he that received seed into the good ground is he that heareth the word, and understandeth it; which also beareth fruit, and bringeth forth, some an hundredfold, some sixty, some thirty. Matthew 13:23

The text indicates that once we hear and *understand* the Word it must bear fruit in our lives. Once the Holy Spirit enlightens our understanding, then application will be the next step, because He will show us how to make the personal application. Fruit bearing therefore means that our lives must reflect the authenticity of the Word, showing its reliability and validity.

The Word argues for a loving God who exists, not distantly, but One who is intimately connected with His children, supplying all of their needs. Thus our lives must reflect the goodness of God to us. That, in essence, is the fruit.... and the fruit must be sweet and nourishing to others! We can then go right on bearing fruit even into old age, as the Word of God intimates in Psalm 92: 12-14 "The righteous shall flourish like the palm tree: he shall grow like a cedar in Lebanon. Those that be planted in the house of the LORD shall flourish in the courts of our God. They shall still bring forth fruit in old age; they shall be fat and flourishing."

Though, I could do with some more fat, I am standing my ground.

****

Standing

---·◈·---

Wherefore let him that thinketh he standeth, take heed lest he fall. There hath no temptation taken you but such as is common to man: but God is faithful, who will not suffer you to be tempted above that ye are able; but will with the temptation also make a way to escape, that ye may be able to bear it. I Corinthians 10:12, 13

I better understand now that there are several different ways we can spiritually stand. In our modern world, many people do their own kind of standing. They won't stand for nonsense. They will stand up for their rights and various causes. But all of our standing must be in God, even when we stand up for 'our rights'.

In 2004, when God revealed to my heart that I would go through the valley of the shadow of death, *standing up*, I could not conceive how such could be accomplished. But as I looked into the Word of God, I saw that, with God, all things are possible. All His biddings are enablings.

God would cause me to *stand still*, so that I could see His salvation. (See Exodus 14:13.) He would allow me to *stand fast* in the faith so that I would not be tottering about and running from *'pillar to post'*, as we say in Bajan.[23] (See 1 Corinthians 16:13) He would permit me to **stand in awe**, as I witnessed incredible supernaturally orchestrated occurrences. (See Psalm 16:13 and Psalm 12:26.) He would show me how to 'put on the whole armour of God' so that I would be able to **stand against** the wiles of the devil. Part of that armour is of course the shield of faith. God's plan for me, and for all of us actually, is to put on, and keep on, the *whole* armour of God. Then we can stand in our times of testing. (See Ephesians 6: 10-13)

Over the past ten years, I have stood. I have stood before all of my classes teaching them, sometimes about life, as we studied our English Literature texts. I have stood functioning as an associate elder in my local church sharing many messages crafted out of my own experiences. The best sermon is the one you are living.

I have stood in the gym squatting with or pushing weights beyond or near to my body weight. I recollect this incident with a chuckle. It is always great to have a sense of humour; it's a medicine! One day, at school, as I was walking along the corridor, a student who remained hidden shouted out loudly, 'Beanstalk!' I smiled because I knew he meant me and was alluding to my slimness. He repeated it quite loudly and possibly expected me to dash madly down the stairs to see who the culprit was. I did not bite the bait but sailed on gaily to my class.

Some folk find it difficult to stand against taunts, jeering, sneering, gossip and ridicule. In our own strength, it would be impossible. But, in God, we can stand against anything. God has made provision for us to stand and not buckle when circumstances in our lives change, for whatever reason.

One Christian writer advises that we as Christians need to examine ourselves and make sure that we are standing *in the*

---

[23] Barbadian dialect

faith. We need to take a good hard look at ourselves, because unless Christ is in us, we are reprobates, mere counterfeits. That may sound hard, but it is true. God can help us all to be genuine to the core so that when we sing "Lord, I want to be a Christian in my heart', it is a heartfelt desire that the Holy Spirit will help us to achieve.

Some people may not engage in introspection, it is easier to spend more time inspecting others. However, we are challenged by the Word of God to take a look at **ourselves**:

> *Examine yourselves to see if your faith is genuine.*
> *Test yourselves. Surely you know that Jesus Christ*
> *is among you; if not, you have failed the test of*
> *genuine faith. 2 Corinthians 13:5 (NLT)*

You can never know your true stance, how strong you are, until you are tested. We must be standing *in Christ,* and not merely *in a church.* The following spiritual advice tells us how we can stand:

> 'Let us plant our feet upon the Rock of Ages and
> then we will have abiding support and consolation.
> Our soul will repose in God with unshaken
> confidence.'[24]

Then our *final standing* will be the one where our eternal destiny is decided. This is indeed a very solemn thought.

> *And I saw the dead, great and small, **standing***
> ***before the throne**, and books were opened.*
> *Another book was opened, which is the book of life.*
> *The dead were judged according to what they had*

---

[24] Ellen G. White, Reflecting Christ, Review and Herald Publishing Association, Hagerstown, MD (1985) p 351

> done as recorded in the books. Revelation 20:12
> (NLT Version)

Some day we shall all stand before our Maker to give an account of how we have lived our lives. We do not need to be afraid of that time as long as we lived our lives *standing in Christ*. As I read Revelation 5 and understood how Jesus will stand for me, I was moved to tears. Read it for yourself and check out Ray Bolt's song *One Drop of Blood*. Once we have stood for Christ in this life, the Lamb will surely stand up for us!

****

Acting on the Word

───────◦❁◦───────

**And Simon answered, Master, we toiled all
night and took nothing! But *at your word,
(according to what you say)* I will let down
the nets. Luke 5:5**

**The nobleman saith unto him, Sir, come down
ere my child die. Jesus saith unto him, Go thy
way; thy son liveth. And the man *believed the
word* that Jesus had spoken unto him, and he
went his way. And as he was now going down,
his servants met him, and told him, saying,
Thy son liveth. John 4: 49-51**

When God gives you 'a Word', it is not an empty promise. God's
Word is based on His character and His authority. A negative
situation changed for the disciples and the nobleman because
they acted on the Word of Jesus. They believed there would
be a difference because Jesus had spoken. I am told that the
written Word is as powerful as the spoken Word. We know that
the spoken Word brought the universe and our tiny planet into
existence!

In 2003 God gave me an initial word as I sought His direction.
It came via my reading. Succinctly put, it was that my Blessed
Advocate had already claimed my answer and I would grieve
and disappoint him if I gave up the conflict the very moment

the victory was on the way to meet me.... and the Spirit was only waiting my trust to whisper in my heart the echo of the answer from the throne that "It is done". The entire message or 'Rhema word' is found in Streams in The Desert July 20 and is documented in a Prayer Letter. In 2003, in my prayer journal, I wrote my response to the message.

Consequently, my entire approach all along my journey, no doubt baffling and inexplicable to some, has been, 'It is done while it is being done.' God dropped a word in my spirit and confirmed it many times over from the Bible. He did not say that I would never die, but that I would *live to declare His praises.*

Inferred in the statement that I should not give up the conflict when the victory was on its way to meet me, is the fact that the journey would be a lengthy one. Yet, in the naivety of my thinking, I was expecting a 'quick fix'. Yes, I certainly wanted to 'hasten my escape from the windy storm *and* tempest'. Psalm 55:12.

I had an opportunity to have my views expressed in the Nation Newspaper on Monday September 26, 2011 in an article captioned, *Believing In Words of Promise.* Facilitated by my colleague, Mrs. Annette Maynard-Watson, she wrote:

> *In conclusion, Mrs. Estwick reinforced that her most significant learning experience was fully understanding that God is a Man of His word. Estwick noted: 'If God says it is done, well then it 'dun'! We can put our neck on the very block of His word and live.'* (See Appendix for the article.)

****

46

Leaning on God's Wisdom

———————•◦❊◦•———————

Trust God from the bottom of your heart; don't try to figure out everything on your own. Listen for God's voice in everything you do, everywhere you go, He's the one who will keep you on track. Don't assume that you know it all. Run to God! Run from evil! Your body will glow with health, your *very bones will vibrate with life! Honor God with everything you own; give him the first and the best. Your barns will burst,* your wine vats will brim over. Proverbs 3: 5 – *10 (Message Bible)*

God always delights to do us good. *He is the Good Shepherd.* However, we would have to ask for and respect the wisdom He offers us in handling various situations. How easy it is to lean on our own understanding. After all, 'we got common sense'.

The catalyst for my adventure was my decision to seek God's advice on whether I should engage in a surgical procedure which was recommended. Was I just being a faith fanatic, a religious freak, wanting to twist God's hands? Was God directing my path, or was I stubbornly pursuing my own way?

If God is truly directing your path, I have discovered that He will sustain you on that path, however difficult it may appear to become. He will never leave you in the lurch. A blessing of trusting God is "marrow to thy bones". What an unusual metaphor. I discovered that the blood is made, of all places, in the bones! God always goes for the root. We tend to focus on the symptoms.

****

Divine Tutoring at Night

I will bless the Lord, who hath given me counsel: my reins also instruct me in the night seasons. Psalms 16:7

I will bless the Lord who advises me; even *at night I am instructed in the depths of my mind. Common English Bible*

Counsel abounds everywhere but there is one kind of counsel that is infallible and that is Divine counsel. It is made available to all of God's children. At night, when we settle down to sleep, the Holy Spirit drops thoughts in our minds, advises us and tells us how to accomplish His will. It was in the "night seasons" that God dropped in my spirit that I would walk through the valley of the shadow of death *standing up.* He used Jeremiah 17: 7, 8 to do it.

I documented my thoughts and the message received in my prayer journal during my quiet time on Friday, January 30, 2004. Were my thoughts proceeding from a "heat oppressed brain" as Shakespeare's Macbeth would say? I asked for confirmation... and received it.

God responded to my request for confirmation in a letter which my friend gave to me that same Friday morning. She knew absolutely nothing of what had transpired the night before. Pastor

Joanna Charles-Greaves, my spiritual sister and friend, handed me her divinely inspired note on the corridor while at school. Strategically timed, she confirmed what I had been previously told 'in the night seasons'. She wrote her impressions from God. Here is the note written almost nine years ago:

> *My Dear Nola,*
>
> *This says your Father: 'My child you shall live and not die, to proclaim my goodness.' (My Insert: see Psalm 118:17) The Lord says: 'I will be like the dew to you my daughter. You shall grow like the lily, and your roots shall lengthen like Lebanon. Your branches shall be those of a spruce tree, they shall spread.*
>
> *Your beauty shall be like an olive tree, and your fragrance like Lebanon. Your family shall be revived like grain and grow like a vine. Their smell shall be like the wine of Lebanon.' Hosea 14: 4-7. Amen*
>
> *"I have confidence that our God will accomplish what concerns you today and every day."*
>
> *Joanna*

Talk about women mentoring women! True Godly women will always function as instruments of blessing in the lives of others, debunking the negative image of women as gossipers and news carriers.

****

50

Walking in Wisdom's Ways

—•❋•—

The fear of the LORD is the beginning of wisdom: and the knowledge of the holy is understanding. For by me thy days shall be multiplied, and the years of thy life shall be increased. Proverbs 9: 10 & 11

The reverent and worshipful fear of the Lord is the beginning (the chief and choice part) of Wisdom, and the knowledge of the Holy One is insight and understanding. For by me [Wisdom from God] your days shall be multiplied, and the years of your life shall be increased. (The Amplified Bible)

Not following God's wisdom can cost you your life. The big irony though, is that folk may think that when you seek God's wisdom on health matters, that you are going to end up being a loser, if not dead! (We will all die someday, except we live until Jesus comes.) However, the feeling which may exist is that when you follow man's advice, all will go well for you. Hmm!

Man's advice has a limit because of our humanity, we are not infallible. Should the truth be spoken, it is easier for us to trust a man that we can see, than a God we cannot see! Implicit trust in God requires at times, a leap in faith, so it will seem risky. We prefer to take our risks with man, God may fail us! (My tongue just got stuck in my cheek.)

The Bible unequivocally makes the point that relying on God's wisdom results in your days being multiplied and years being added to your life. One can logically assume that the opposite can then occur. Your life can be shortened by following the wrong advice. It is very true that there is a way that seems right unto a man but the ends thereof are the ways of death. Can we die *before* our time? Certainly!

A Christian writer makes the point that we rob our families, our communities, our churches and God Himself of our service when we die *before our time*. Personally, I think before your time refers to departing this earth before you have completed the specific assignment God has ordained for you to do, one written in your book of life, even before you were born. (See Jeremiah 1:5) Such divine strategy could not be limited to one human being. Maybe we need a quantum leap in our thinking to fathom such an idea. The ultimate purpose of our lives cannot be mere church attendance. We need to stretch our minds to the larger purpose. I am 'stretched out'.

****

Walking in Your Own Sparks

———— ·❂· ————

Behold, all ye that kindle a fire, that compass yourselves about with sparks: walk in the light of your fire, and in the sparks that ye have kindled. This shall ye have of mine hand; ye shall lie down in sorrow. Isaiah 50:11

This is a very powerful text. It jumped out at me one day with such lucidity! Thankfully, following God's wisdom has its own checks and balances. Sometimes onlookers may speculate that we are stupid, doing "bare ignorance" as we would say in Bajan dialect. The Word of God is very powerfully predictive in Isaiah 50:11.

The imagery in the text really refers to handling matters in the way you think is best. Ostensibly, you may have prayed. But the truth is that many folk may 'pray' and then go and do just as they please with little reference to God. The 'prayer' is entirely cosmetic. In essence then, we follow our wisdom; our own common sense directs us. Therefore, we walk in our own sparks.

All of this can be done while verbally *talking* about following God's direction. We veer from God's path, and imperceptibly, we are walking in our own way. I think a major variable when it comes to matters of health is the fear of death. We may choose a path, seeking to avoid death, only to hear the hollow laugh of the grim reaper.

It is not God's intention that we lie down in sorrow. Neither does He want us to be like the woman who spent all her savings on doctors. But far from being made better, ironically, she was worse. (See Luke 8:43-48) The result of lying down in sorrow is not some arbitrarily imposed situation, but would more come as a result of God respecting our choices.

I firmly believe that whichever way you choose, God will be with you and will comfort you. It may not have been His intention for you to lie in torment but God will never force His will upon us! Sometimes God's wisdom may look like foolishness but as He is the very epitome of wisdom, we could never expect the proverbial fox to outwit its Maker. Now, could we? Psalm 25:3 is a text of assurance: "No one who waits for You will ever be put to shame, but all who are unfaithful will be put to shame." (God's Word Translation)

****

More Clever Than a Fox

*Oh, the depth of the riches both of the wisdom
and knowledge of God! How unsearchable are
His judgments and unfathomable His ways!
Romans 11:33*

*With Him are wisdom and might; To Him
belong counsel and understanding" Job 12:13.*

We are all endowed with some measure of common sense. But common sense is not synonymous with wisdom. In fact, I am told that common sense is not so common after all. Plus, there is man's wisdom, but then, there is *God's wisdom*, which admittedly, looks like utter madness at times.

Whoever would imagine any logic whatsoever, in a group of people marching around Jericho city for seven days and then seven times on the seventh day, as a way of bringing down the city's walls? Additionally, the people were to be utterly silent in their march until they were commanded to shout loudly. The walls actually fell. Read the exciting narrative in Joshua 6:1-27.

Then there was that time that an army went out to battle and King Jehoshaphat sent the choir out before the army. So, if anyone would be slaughtered first, it would be the poor choir members. Were we back there, we might have contracted a sudden cold. Going into battle singing!! Preposterous! But, a resounding victory was secured. Read that amazing account in 2 Chronicles 20.

Who does not know of Gideon, who at God's instructions, went out to fight a massive army of thousands, with only three hundred men? Now, that looked absolutely suicidal. However, Gideon was following the instructions God gave him. The Bible tells us the results of that radical obedience. See Judges Chapter 7 for a full account.

So let's bring God's wisdom into the 21st century. These are critical points to note: God speaks to each of us individually on matters that relate to important choices we may have to make. God's directions do not often square with human logic. He is outside the box of our human thinking.

God will never force His way upon us, He will always leave us with a choice and even with some room for doubt. His way of solving some matters may be quite simple, so simple that it may even seem ridiculous. What Mary told the servants at the wedding in Cana must become our mandate as well: Whatsoever he saith unto you, do it. John 2:5.

Our obedience to God's individualized instructions to us may seem to bring us into trouble, even appearing to precipitate our untimely end. But the Bible says that unto *God* belong the issues of life and death. (See Psalm 68:20)

It is to be noted that the Bible makes a striking correlation between following God's wisdom and a lengthening of one's days.

> *Happy is the man who finds wisdom, and the man*
> *who gains understanding; length of days is in her*
> *right hand... Her ways are ways of pleasantness,*

and all her paths are peace. She is a tree of life to
those who take hold of her, and happy are all who
retain her. Proverbs 3: 13 & 16-18.

We are talking about lengthening of days, not God's promise of immortality. That promise will be fulfilled at His second coming. So, someday, unless we live to see Jesus coming in the clouds, we shall all die. *God* knows the number of our days. Yet, it would seem to me that there is a human tendency to put people on death row and to number their days. Of course, there is what is known as dramatic irony. To keep this insert as short as possible, please 'google' that literary term. Note that God would be the omniscient audience.

With a sense of humour that will not be squelched, I penned one of my favourite poems in 2005. Slightly satirical in nature, and written in Bajan dialect, I think it is a memorable creation. I still chuckle at it. I have often noted that though I am a rather quiet person, I am not foolish. Quietness and stupidity are not synonymous!

The poem is intended to establish the fact that we can be truly ignorant; lacking in information and knowledge, and not even know it. In the realm of health, if I have a teachable spirit my ignorance (lack of life-saving knowledge) can be corrected. However, ignorance and arrogance (a proud, 'know-it-all' and unteachable attitude) can be quite a lethal combination!

When all is said and done, God's ways and wisdom are inscrutable! We dare not question them. In Standard English the title of the poem is: They are waiting. However, I think you may prefer:

Duh Waiting

Yes, duh waiting fuh me to collapse
Not a malicious desire but a vague expectation
Cause I step out de box and could be wrong
Blaps! Drop down to de ground
Me and my faith reduced to a poor pitiful mound.
Wuh she playing doh?
Talking bout God lead she pun some other path
Wuh law! I got to laugh
Cause some people does 'car' dis religion ting too far
Duh wishing pun a star
Cuh dear, God gi we common sense
At nuh expense
So we en got to ask He to direct we here and dere
We got sense enough we own self to steer.

Hmmm! well lemme tell dum sum ting
I as blind as a bat.
So I got to ask God: 'Which way to turn? Dis or dat?
Plus, he dun tell me if ya lack wisdom, 'Ask me,
I does give it way fuh free'
Some people real wise and know wuh to do
But I tell yah, duh en got a clue!
Duh tie up in a box
Dem en know that God smarter and more
clever than the proverbial fox!!

Leh dum wait and "wizzy wizzy"
But my God and I busy busy!!!
Doing dixie in de valley
"Come," He says, 'Leh we dally!
I hay standing still
Cause God routing de enemy
Every promise He gun fulfill
He dun say in de Word dat

Dem who dare to wait pun He
He gun make all duh enemies flee
He say deh en gun be confounded
In fact, the skeptics and agnostics
will be left astounded
So leh dum wait
Tinking duh know my fate
Yeah... right!
Nola... de late!
Leh dum wait fuh me to collapse
Brax!
De rocking chair of peace God put me in
Is a cool place to relax!
When ya dare to obey God's Rhema Word to ya heart
Expect de talk to start
But sistah, don doubt! God does finish wuh ever He start.
Once God in de canoe wid you
De rapids you will ford with dexterity and finesse
Cause God doan mess
He will rain down and bless
All a we who prepared to stan de test!!!

Composed by Nola Estwick
November 27, 2005

****

Peace Like A River

What man is he that feareth the LORD? Him shall he teach in the way that he shall choose. His soul shall dwell at ease; and his seed shall inherit the earth. Psalm 25: 12 & 13

The secret of the LORD is with them that fear him; and he will shew them his covenant. Psalm 25:14

I like this rendering of Psalm 25:14: The secret [of the sweet, satisfying companionship] of the Lord have they who fear (revere and worship) Him, and He will show them His covenant and reveal to them its [deep, inner] meaning. AMP

This is what the Lord says— your Redeemer, the Holy One of Israel: "I am the Lord your God, who teaches you what is good for you and leads you along the paths you should follow. Oh, that you had listened to my commands! Then you would have had peace flowing like a gentle river and righteousness rolling over you like waves in the sea. Isaiah 48:17 & 18 (NLT)

The above verses contain some profound messages!! One powerful literary device the Bible uses is *contrast*. As we juxtapose texts, we see more clearly the powerful messages which God wants us to understand. Psalm 25:12-14 clearly delineate the benefits of fearing or trusting God. 'What is the man that fearest God?' In other words the psalmist seems to be saying, 'Show me someone who trusts God. Such a person, God will personally teach the way he should choose.'

I respectfully told a medical practitioner at a point in my health and faith adventure that we are not clones. God deals with each of us differently. The recounting of my journey has never been intended to be prescriptive. I am merely being *descriptive*.

Getting back on target, for the person who trusts God, the Word says that his soul will dwell at ease. In other words, he will not be panic-stricken and cowering in fear. Some years ago, I wrote a poem called *Inside of Me*. The terrain inside of me has never changed: a peaceful stream meandering through verdant pastures, as I sit beside still waters. (See Psalm 23)

But there is the other side of the picture. In Isaiah 48:18 I can almost hear God saying in plaintive tones: 'I am so sorry that you did not go the way I had laid out for you, if only you had done that... then you would have had all of my peace.' Note the conditional element in the text: '*You would have had*'. While we like to simplify the responses of God to our requests by saying that He says: 'Yes, no or wait,' it is not always that simple. There are certainly other variables to consider. We dare not make God a cosmic scapegoat for all of our seemingly unanswered prayers.

The often overlooked variable is that of meeting the conditions of *answered* prayer. And it does not always have to do with faith or lack of it. It may simply be that we make a crucial decision based on insufficient information. We may not realize it until we are solidly along the path and reversal is well-nigh difficult. I contend that God is always with us, no matter what. He says that He will never leave us nor forsake us. (Hebrews 13:5)

I love the thought which comes from Psalm 25. God will reveal His secrets to the person who trusts in Him. God will tell us what others do not know. And finally, this must be our aspiration:

> *...Everyone needs to have a personal experience in obtaining a knowledge of the will of God. We must individually hear Him speaking to the heart. When every other voice is hushed, and in quietness we wait before Him, the silence of the soul makes more distinct the voice of God. He bids us, '**Be still, and know that I am God.**' Ps. 46:10*[25]

Has God ever told *you* a secret in the very depths of your soul? Or, are you so busy, even doing laudable church duties, that you are just too busy to be still and listen? God never whispers 'sweet nothings'. I love His secrets. They make for a life of adventure with Him!

****

---

[25] Ellen G. White, *The Desire of Ages*, Pacific Press Publishing Association, Mountain View, California, (1898), p. 363

Rejoicing Over Us

————— ⚜ —————

*And I will make an everlasting covenant with
them, that I will not turn away from them, to
do them good; but I will put my fear in their
hearts, that they shall not depart from me.
Yea, I will rejoice over them to do them good,
and I will plant them in this land assuredly
with my whole heart and with my whole soul.
Jeremiah 32:40, 41*

Before there was any awareness that there would be a storm on
the horizon of my life, these texts were supernaturally given to me
at a Women Ministries session in early 2003. The providential
details are documented in one of the prayer letters. At the
appropriate time God impressed on my heart: 'The message is
for now.'

When I first received those texts they seemed to bear no
relevance to me whatsoever. As the Holy Spirit showed me how
to personalize this Rhema word, I came to understand what
God was telling me. His message was that He would put His
fear in my heart that I would not depart from Him. That means
that He would cause my love for Him to intensify. As a result, I
would understand His revealed purposes and happily submit, not
harboring a spirit of resentment or resignation. For underneath
that spirit of resignation, which could *appear t*o be submission,
there can be anger and discontent, camouflaged however with

the 'right words'. God alone sees right into the very depths of our hearts and knows *the truth*!

There has never been a flicker of a moment of any rebellion in my heart against God, any questioning of His plan. In fact, I told God that even if I became as thin as a pin, I would never stop trusting Him, but then I turned around and said in Bajan parlance: 'But God, ah din intend fuh yah to tek muh seriously doh.' (In Standard English: 'God, I did not intend for you to take me seriously though.') We chuckled heartily. God understands Bajan, though He is not one, as some Bajans seem to feel!!

So, for me now to 'get an attitude' because God decides to test me would be sheer madness! It would be like throwing away over thirty years of walking in a very satisfying fellowship and camaraderie with the God of my youth. In fact, one could even question my *motives* for claiming to be a Christian. God made a covenant with me to do me good and plant me in the land and well... how I have grown! Cedars in Lebanon are tall and strong. I am still growing... My growth would have been stunted if God did not hide me...

****

Hidden by God

———•◉•———

Keep me as the apple of the eye, hide me under the shadow of thy wings. Psalms 17:8

For in the time of trouble he shall hide me in his pavilion: in the secret of his tabernacle shall he hide me; he shall set me up upon a rock. Psalms 27:5

Thou shalt be hid from the scourge of the tongue: neither shalt thou be afraid of destruction when it cometh. Job 5:21

I could never have survived the last ten years if God had not hidden me. Hidden under His wings, I continue to safely abide, in the midst of any storm. Set on a rock, God raised me above the foes which can sap the human spirit: fear, doubt, anxiety and all their pesky cousins. Hidden in His pavilion, I did not fall prey to depression or despondency as I saw my weight undulating. God also protected me from the poison of the tongue. The Psalmist David himself, prayed to be protected from what, can at times, be quite a venomous organ:

Hide me from the secret counsel of the wicked; from the insurrection of the workers of iniquity: Who whet their tongue like a sword, and bend their bows to shoot their arrows, even bitter words: That they

> *may shoot in secret at the perfect: suddenly do they*
> *shoot at him, and fear not. Psalm 64: 2-4*

I was indeed miraculously hidden from the scourge of the tongue. It is certainly untrue to say, 'Sticks and stones may break my bones but words would never hurt me.' Words can, and do hurt. Fortunately, I do not have any friends who would bring me gossip. Anything I heard was 'by the way', purely coincidental. Some folk apparently felt that 'someone should talk to me'. Thank God, He protected me from all the 'Job's Comforters' who wanted to 'knock common sense in my head'. Though I became mildly aware of some negative comments which swirled around me, the words had no power, by the grace of the living God, to affect my spirit.

I must admit that I pondered whether the 'enemies of faith', had *they* been called to walk through the valley of the shadow of death, *standing up,* would have been able to walk with the same stamina, pluck, focus, determination and fortitude, as God alone, has enabled me to do. I did not give myself any of the necessary 'accoutrements' for a long journey. None of them reside innately in me. They are all God-given.

Indeed, we can *never know* what it means to 'walk a mile in a person's shoes', unless we actually do it. And, *we cannot,* as the term is merely metaphorical! Our loving Heavenly Father hides His children from those who would come to discourage them. But God *never hides* from those who will trust in Him. Wow! That's great!

> *For he hath not despised nor abhorred the affliction*
> *of the afflicted; neither hath he hid his face from him;*
> *but when he cried unto him, he heard. Psalm 22:24*

What a blessed assurance to know that God hides us but never hides *from us*!

****

Abundant Fruit

---·•❊•·---

"But blessed is the man who trusts me, God, the *woman who sticks with God. They're like trees replanted in Eden, putting down roots near the rivers—Never a worry through the hottest of summers, never dropping a leaf, Serene and calm through droughts, bearing fresh fruit every season. Jeremiah 17: 7 & 8 The Message Bible*

This very powerful text also constitutes what I call my "Rhema word". This is a special word God gives to His child concerning a situation. It can also be considered as a kind of divine fiat. A fiat is an arbitrary decree or pronouncement, especially by a person or group of persons having absolute authority to enforce it.

God is not arbitrary, neither is He tyrannical. But He can speak a word in our lives. He can tell us that something will happen and then *with our cooperation*, make it come to pass. My understanding, as I meditated on this text that night in 2004, was that I would continue to function in the midst of my health adventure, calm and cool and would continue to yield fruit. (See John 15:5)

The metaphors found in these texts are very striking when deeply contemplated. The man who trusts in God is likened to a tree and such a tree does not change because circumstances change.

In a drought, we would expect vegetation to dry up. Spiritually, a drought would refer to a test or trial or some difficult circumstance. But even in the midst of such circumstances 'her leaf remains green'. There is no anxiety in the 'drought period' and ironically such a tree never ceases from yielding fruit. The Bible is not giving us a treatise on trees but is being very descriptive of the person who is walking through a period of testing or as some may say "adversity".

My journey has been a very fruitful one: Fruit in the scores of appointments with my SDA church family, as well as appointments with brothers and sisters of various denominations. There has also been fruit in various newspaper articles. The article in the Nation's Betterhealth Magazine, the December 2011 issue is one of the most memorable. **(See Appendix)**

There has been fruit in encouragement to those who walked in the valley... and are now peacefully at rest. Well over forty persons. It has been fruit, not mere leaves... fruit! Pruning is one sure way to enable a tree to produce more fruit. When God applies the pruning shears, it is always for our growth. If we want to be more fruitful, producing fruit for the nourishment of others, and not mere leaves there will be a cost attached.

God does not intend for us to be like the barren fig tree, luxuriant foliage but no fruit. Empty impressiveness! The accuracy of God's Word is astounding. He is truly a Divine Strategist par excellence!!! How I praise my Heavenly Dad! I am now a female Bartimaeus. No one can shut me up. I will bellow all the more! Did I hear someone say: 'Be quiet'? If we have something worthwhile to shout about, then we have to shout out!

Many years ago I heard Pastor Ricardo Selman loudly admonish women to keep silent in church if they had nothing worthwhile to say. He paused as if that would have been the end of his comment. I cringed in discomfort thinking he would sure offend the women gathered at that Women Ministry session. But he did not end there. He acknowledged that women do have a lot to share and must not be timid in sharing how God has blessed them. So I will acknowledge that this publication and the one to follow is about shouting out. No turning back now! I am constrained to 'shout out' the goodness of God. Go ahead! You can do it too!

****

Cost Attached

And there went great multitudes with him: and he turned, and said unto them, if any man come to me, and hate not his father, and mother, and wife, and children, and brethren, and sisters, yea, and his own life also, he cannot be my disciple. And whosoever doth not bear his cross, and come after me, cannot be my disciple. For which of you, intending to build a tower, sitteth not down first, and counteth the cost, whether he have sufficient to finish it? Luke 14: 25-28

I have learnt that to everything there is a cost attached. There is even a cost attached to not respecting the body God has given to each one of us. This may be done either ignorantly or deliberately, when we take the greatest treasure we have, our health, for granted. When health becomes compromised in any way, most people, if not all, want instant repair at the cheapest cost possible. But there is work, effort, discipline and self-denial involved in recovering health, particularly by natural means. It will cost us something.

In the spiritual realm, there is a cost attached to the things which we desire as well. James and John went to Jesus making a request. They wanted prominent seats in Jesus' kingdom. (See John 10: 35-40.) Jesus asked whether they would be able to drink His cup or be baptized with His baptism. Naively so, they replied yes.

So with us, we ask God to give us a deeper experience in Him. We ask to be made more Christ like. We ask for faith and all the fruits of the Spirit, which are legally ours. But are they simply for the taking? Does God just drop them out of Heaven on us, as we saunter gaily along on our Christian walk?

No! There is a cost attached. If we want to acquire these precious attributes, the cost attached is the full and complete surrender, without any reservations whatsoever, of our entire life to God. It's an 'all or none' type of surrender. Yes, it will be costly, but yet the rewards will so far outweigh the costs, that what we 'sacrifice' will in fact be almost paltry.

We have to give God leeway to do as He pleases, as typified by the third woman, in the story found in February 9, of *Streams in the Desert*.

The mechanism by which God develops these qualities in us, faith being a foundational one, is the tests and trials of life. So we had better forget about bellyaching, 'Why me?' We need to thank God that He sees something in us that He can work with for our betterment, and even for His glory.

One spiritual writer says that our purification cannot be made complete without our suffering. So, yes, we may go through painful experiences. But it is God's intention that we find all of our strength in Him. Very often it is our attitude which prevents us from sucking honey out of the 'flinty rock' and being refreshed by the streams God will place in our desert areas. (See Deuteronomy 32:13 and Isaiah 41:18)

I fully understand that it is God's plan that we be enriched by our experiences. Whatever we would have lost, or appeared to have lost, God is able to so sufficiently and abundantly supply all of our needs, that we actually need not feel deprived or 'set upon' by the vagaries of our life.

Our human nature would lead us to seek the easy way out of everything. Not only that, we want the best out of God but want to give Him very little. We desire the crown but not the cross. We want a marvellous testimony but we would say to God: 'Please Lord, leave me in my glass case, go test someone else.' We are then left with impressive flowery words to share, but there is really no real crucible experience to back picturesque speech.

When we consider that there is a very high cost attached to our personal eternal salvation, I think we could never ever utter a word of reproach against God. Grace may be free but it is certainly not cheap.

Once we have truly met God, the real God, not a caricature, we will come to see that what we regarded as assets in life, might actually have been liabilities, and what seemed to have been liabilities, were in reality our greatest assets. The Christian life is replete with paradoxes and ironies, which are not readily discernible to the logical and pragmatic thinkers. However, these apparent incongruities are more clearly seen by those who, only with God's help, can look beyond the natural and the apparent. That is exactly what Moses had to do which allowed him to make the right decision. See Hebrews 11 and 2 Corinthians 4:18.

I have never forgotten a conversation, occurring over 30 years ago, which I had with a former colleague. It centred on Matthew 13:44. Here Jesus likens the Kingdom of God to a man who discovered treasure hidden in a field. Wanting the treasure, he decided to sell all that he had in order to purchase the field. We talked about the implications and meaning of the illustration. There was a cost attached to acquiring that field. The treasure in that field really represented Jesus, who is symbolised as the Pearl of Great Price.

Since the implication was obvious to my colleague, he told me point blank, that God was asking too much. To give up all for Jesus was just too much. I guess 'all' for him meant he would have been deprived of a good life. How utterly ironic!

Is it conceivable that God could ask too much of us? Is the cost attached to surrender too high? Unwittingly, my colleague, at that point in his life, may have been like the young man who came to Jesus with a desire to follow Him, until Jesus told him the conditions. When he heard the 'cost attached', he turned sadly away.

I thank God that the riches of His grace far outweigh any cost attached! God is a superb accountant and His books will always balance. We can never lose with God; we can never come up short. Far from coming up short, God will so open the windows of Heaven that we will not have room enough for our bounties. When God showers His blessings on us, we can afford to lavishly share our wealth. Our God is not some parsimonious, tight fisted mean old scrooge. If such a God exists, *I have never met Him.* Anyone who wants to quibble about cost should have a look at Calvary!

I would advise anyone to simply unleash himself with God, no matter the cost, you will not end up impoverished but greatly enriched. See for yourself! I think I have an extra pair of glasses.

Count You in For a Purging?

I am the true vine, and my Father is the husbandman. Every branch in me that beareth not fruit he taketh away: and every branch that beareth fruit, he purgeth it, that it may bring forth more fruit. John 15: 1 & 2

Some of us as adults would remember our days as children when we were forced to take castor oil. Not a pleasant affair! In the spiritual realm, God also does His own purging, but it does not send us running to the bathroom. Such purging is designed to clean up our hearts and allow us to bear more fruit. The word pruning is often substituted for purging. God prunes those branches which are in Him and are already bearing fruit. Pruning involves pain. For the physical process, if the plant could talk, it might emit a bewildered scream and wonder why the gardener was chopping at him in such a seemingly ruthless manner. Plants don't talk, but we as humans do.

What will we say and do during our pruning/purging time? Will we even recognize it as such? Some who have boasted of great faith and confidence in God in the days of sunshine and even merrily and mindlessly repeated: 'God is good all the time, and all the time God is good' may start, under pressure, to accuse God of being mean, unfair, harsh, unkind and insensitive.

Of course, this will not be done openly, but secretly and insidiously, through their 'innocent' questions such as: "Why me?", "Can God furnish a table for me in the wilderness?" "Has God forsaken me?" I can almost hear the rebuttals being formed to hurl at me. But wait a minute! Innocent and 'human' as those questions may appear, they actually strike at the character of God. They subtly question His dealings with us and can pave the way for flagrant rebellion. I quite like the timely counsel that one of my favourite spiritual writers gives:

The pruning will cause pain, but it is the Father who applies the knife. He works with no wanton hand or indifferent heart.[26]

Please read the entire chapter which sets the quotation within a context. The book may be accessed on line. See: http://www. ellenwhite.info/books/ellen-g-white-book-desire-of-ages-da-73. htm. It is Chapter 73: *Let not your heart be troubled.*

I was absolutely amazed in my spiritual reading, to have discovered a truth, which I have experienced in my journey. Maybe, it has happened to you. You read something and realize that the writer has unwittingly documented what you have known from a practical perspective. I have reflected: 'Well I am okay. I am not so crazy after all.'

The branch that is in Christ must expect to be pruned. Spiritual writer Ellen White says:

> *When affliction and disappointment come, you are to show altogether a different character of fruit than the world. There is the evidence that you are connected with Jesus Christ, and there is a power that sustains you in all your afflictions,*

---

[26] Ellen G. White, *The Desire of Ages*, Pacific Press Publishing Association, 1350 Villa Street, Mountain View, California 94042, (1898) p 677

> disappointments and trials; and this power and
> grace sweetens every affliction. When the cup of
> suffering may be placed to your lips, there is a
> Comforter and Helper. The cup of consolation is
> placed in the hand, **and it may be the happiest
> period of your life.** *(My* emphasis.*)* [27]

It seems incongruous to be in a situation of trial and test and yet that time is the happiest period of your life. I have never felt more fulfilled and in sync with God's plan for my life than now. I have truly enjoyed my various appointments with groups and individuals, as God has orchestrated those meetings. I have enjoyed my deep internal mutter chats with God as we have chuckled at some things. I concur with the words of a song which says: 'The miles of my journey have proved my God true.'

Just recently, 'Jack' on seeing me, asked, 'How are you doing?' I replied 'I am excellent, by God's grace.' The look which spread over Jack's face caused me to chuckle. Of course, I could not read his thoughts but his facial response spoke. Jack is going through his time of challenge and having heard me speak publicly, as well as having read a few of the Prayer Letters, he may find my response incongruous. 'How can she be so positive and happy?' There are possibly many such 'Jacks'. Often the assumptions we make about a person, will dictate our response to him/her.

I think the incongruity of being happy at your most testing time could only be possible if there is truly an 'abiding in the Vine'. The terms 'abiding in the Vine' and being 'in Christ' are actually synonymous. I believe that those terms refer to the personal relationship with God which each of us is privileged to enjoy. This is a relationship where you liaise with God on everything. You would talk with Him naturally and regularly about all that

[27] Ellen G. White, *Reflecting Christ*. Review and Herald Publishing Association, Hagerstown, MD (1985) p 355

concerns you, much in the same way that you would chit chat with your best friend.

You are completely happy and relaxed with God. There's no continual fighting and struggling with Him on issues, where you are tugging against His will. Your attitude is not one of stress and anxiety, but one of complete peace and calm. Many years ago, I came across a very deep comment which became embedded in my consciousness. I see this spiritual exposition as representing the zenith of the Christian experience. As long as God can mature us to that point in our friendship with Him, then we can become spiritual millionaires. Here is the comment:

> *All true obedience comes from the heart. It was heart work with Christ. And if we consent, He will so identify Himself with our thoughts and aims, so blend our hearts and minds into conformity to His will, that when obeying Him we shall be but carrying out our own impulses. The will, refined and sanctified, will find its highest delight in doing His service. When we know God as it is our privilege to know Him, our life will be a life of continual obedience.*[28]

'When obeying Him, we shall be but carrying out our own impulses.' Have you caught the depth of that idea? When I apply it personally, it means that what I want to do, is also what God wants me to do, and what God wants me to do is just what I want to do. That must be bliss! To have such an experience would be a very worthwhile objective, for then, and only then, would we be able to obey the paradoxical instruction given in James 1:2. So, are you ready to count it all joy when the pruning process starts?

****

---

[28] Ellen G. White, *The Desire of Ages*, Pacific Press Publishing Association, 1350 Villa Street, Mountain View, California 94042, (1898) p 688

A New Song

---·❖·---

And he hath put a new song to sing, a hymn of praise to our God. Many will see what he has done and be amazed. They will put their trust in the LORD. Psalm 40: 3 (NLT Version)

God has indeed put a new song in my mouth. I can now venture beyond the bathroom walls. In the Bible, spectacular occasions were often celebrated with songs. The Israelites sang their new song *after* they had crossed the Red Sea. The song must have been written either before they crossed over, or extemporaneously composed, on the shores upon their exit. Someone said that they sang the song on the *wrong side* of the Red Sea. I am writing my song and singing it at the same time. I am not waiting for the climax of my journey. Singing while on the journey sweetens the melody!

Very memorable is my divinely orchestrated appointment with an audience of Moravian singers and musicians on February 11, 2006. Arranged by Rev. Mikie Roberts and Rev. Marlene Britton-Walfall, my topic was: 'Called to Sing in the Valley of The Shadow of Death.' I had an absolute ball with these wonderful exuberant Christians. Indeed, an appointment never to be forgotten! I dedicated an entire prayer letter to recounting my moment in time with my Moravian brothers and sisters.

The song of my life has no minor notes. It is not a dirge. It is a song of praise and I believe many are seeing it and more will see it. What a beautiful end result: we shall all trust God more!

****

A Sacrifice of Praise

••❀••

The LORD is my strength and my shield;
my heart trusted in him, and I am helped:
therefore my heart greatly rejoiceth; and with
my song will I praise him. Psalm 28:7

It is relatively easy to give praise to God when there is salubrious weather. The test of faith is really to be able maintain a paean of praise to God when the weather of our life changes and we are buffeted by storms of various kinds. The concept of the sacrifice of praise speaks to those times when, left to operate in our carnal human nature, we may grumble and fret. Some may argue that such a response is unavoidable. I would very highly recommend reading the book: *The God of all Comfort,* by Hannah Whitall-Smith, to be given a paradigm shift in that kind of thinking. Chapters three and four would be particularly helpful. The entire book may be accessed on line.

Having an understanding that God has a wonderful plan for our life, which will include tests, will enable us to honour Him, unflinchingly declaring His goodness, even when it may appear to others that something 'bad' is occurring in our lives.

Jesus can give us songs in the night. One of the most therapeutic ways of boosting our immune system is actually through songs of praise to God. I have had many great songs to cheer me on my journey of faith in God. Not only must songs of praise come from our lips but our lives should be a litany of praise to God. It is easier to sing the lofty lyrics of songs but so much harder to live the words.

A few mornings ago, as soon as I awoke, a verse of a song was deposited in my mind, no doubt by my Friend, The Holy Spirit. He often speaks quietly to the inner ear. The song is *Day By Day* and it is number 532 in the SDA church hymnal. The message which impressed itself upon me is that as His child, God takes special responsibility for my care. That reinforcement was gratefully received as I can still see the veins in my hands like the gnarled knotted roots of a tree.

Understanding and being able to live the words of this song would make a tremendous difference in our Christian experience, especially when the terrain of the road changes and becomes a little bumpy. Here are a few lines from the song:

> Help me then in every tribulation
> So to trust Thy promises, O Lord,
> That I lose not faith's sweet consolation
> Offered me within Thy Holy Word.

We sing asking God to help us to trust His promises in every trial, but when the rubber meets the road, is that what we actually do? If the truth is to be spoken, most of us do not look to the promises of God, instead, we look to circumstances and our own weakness and inability. If we did in fact, look to the Word of God and stand upon those mighty promises, God would give us, not one song, but many songs, so that we can give Him endless praise. Our faith would bring us indeed 'sweet consolation'.

In my quiet time, I sometimes sing songs to God. At times a line from a song pops in my mind and I say 'God, this is for you. This is how I feel about You.' Recently the words of this song came to me: "I'll walk with God from this day on. His helping hand I'll lean upon." It is a beautiful song with lovely lyrics. The entire song may be accessed on line. There is a secular song which I have turned into my special song to God. Normally, the lyrics would refer to another human being. However, there is no human being to whom I could say those words, not even my dear hubby, whom I love very much, and who has been an excellent companion over the last thirty two years of our marriage.

Our truest songs of praise must really be to our Divine Husband because God should be number one in our affections. No one should rival Him. When I heard the song, I thought: 'Wow Lord, that is just what I would say to you.' It's an old 'goldie' with which you may be familiar.

> Only you can make this world seem right
> Only you can make the darkness bright
> Only you and you alone can thrill me like you do
> and fill my heart with love for only you.

It is incongruous that your heart could be excited about God and you are thrilled with Him and yet be in the depths of misery. Sometimes when difficulties arise, some folk go to other human beings seeking what only God can give them. The Word tells us to delight ourselves *in the Lord* and admonishes us to let our expectation be from Him. (See Psalm 37:4 and Psalm 62:5)

One thing is certain, it is not possible to be enveloped in self-pity and still be genuinely praising God. How I thank God that I was kept safe from that mangy mongrel. He would have infected me with his sores and I would have been spending time 'licking my wounds' rather than delighting myself in the Lord. Sometimes, an individual may get derailed by that little thieving cur called self-pity who masquerades as a kind sympathiser, 'Oh, poor thing', and he cunningly steals away the blessings God has prepared for that person, even in the midst of tests.

As we trust the promises of God, they are strong enough to keep our feet unswervingly on the narrow road of faith. We need not falter a decibel in our praise to God even if life, for some reason, should become tempestuous. By a self-abandoned reliance on the promises of God's Word, we can certainly discover the accuracy of Martin Luther's famous words: 'A mighty fortress is our God, a bulwark never failing'. With God as our fortress and bulwark, we are enabled to bring into the house of the Lord our unique 'sacrifice of praise'!

Strong to Do Exploits

───────── ◆ ─────────

The LORD is good, a strong hold in the day of trouble; and he knoweth them that trust in him. Nahum 1:7

Also rendered: The LORD is good – a refuge in troubled times. He knows those who are confiding in him. ISV

...But the people that do know their God shall be strong, and do exploits. Daniel 11:32

Man looks at the outward appearance but God looks at the heart. As I meditated on Nahum 1:8, the idea of being 'short listed' was impressed upon me. Only God knows those who *truly trust* Him, as opposed to those who *say* that they do. The day of trouble will reveal the truth. The list of talkers will always be longer than the list of walkers. So the question we must ask ourselves is: "Am I short listed?" Those who are short listed and know God experientially will be strong and do great things. Knowing God makes all the difference to our level of strength and the extent of our spiritual achievements.

Incredibly, I can put my hand on a presentation I gave at a Women's Ministries Award Ceremony on Sunday July 14, 2001. I was asked to deliver the feature address and the theme boldly emblazoned on the wall behind me was: "He Has Done Great

Things." In attendance was Mrs. Esmee Branner, author of the book 'Beyond The Veil'. She was our guest speaker for the weekend. May I share a snippet of what I said on that evening, eleven years ago:

> *If we could stretch this theme out to its limits we would see that the term great things encompasses what God can accomplish in us in terms of our character development, what He can accomplish through transforming us into instruments of blessing to others and through expanding our borders of ministry...*

As I continued to explore the theme through examining the lives of Mary the mother of Jesus and Mary Magdalene I noted:

> *Neither of these women allowed what others would think of them to limit them. Mary Jesus' mother knew that Jesus' supernatural birth would cause some tongues to wag, but she unhesitatingly surrendered to the will of God. Mary Magdalene, propelled by a deep love for Jesus, also opened herself up to ridicule when she did something so outrageously unorthodox, as letting down her hair and washing the feet of Jesus with her tears.* Her desire was to please her Lord, not to look good in the eyes of others. May God always give us the courage to follow the convictions of our hearts!!

One might say: 'Be careful what you say, because you may be given opportunity to back the talk by the walk.' But then again as Christians we should welcome opportunities to have our talk substantiated by our walk. People tend to watch the walk more than listen to the talk and they should see consistency.

****

A Man of His Word

---◦◉◦---

God is not a man, that he should lie; neither the son of man, that he should repent: hath he said, and shall he not do it? Or hath he spoken, and shall he not make it good? Numbers 23:19

This text has been in my arsenal for many years. I simply love it. It was riveted in my heart many years ago as I sat on the Oistins beach, surveying the vast expanse of the sea, while I quietly contemplated the awesomeness of God and His power. The big issue really boils down to God's character. If you do not really know God, experientially, you will be unable to trust Him. (See Psalm 34:8) If you have never tasted Him, *really tasted Him, then you cannot know how soul satisfying He is, especially in the storm!!* Some aspects of God's character are discovered only as you closely interact with Him and His word in the nitty-gritty affairs of life.

You will never put your life into the hands of someone with whom you have a mere passing acquaintance. There is no argument whatsoever about that. Once you believe in the depths of your soul that the God *you know*, does not tell lies, does not renege on His promises, is not double dealing, then you can freely trust Him and walk through any valley, desert or storm, with your head held high ... *and even whistle a happy tune!*

****

Being a Pilgrim

---·❀·---

Blessed is the man whose strength is in thee; in whose heart are the ways of them. Who passing through the valley of Baca make it a well; the rain also filleth the pools. They go from strength to strength; every one of them in Zion appeareth before God. Psalm 84: 4-7

Life is a pilgrimage toward the special reason for which each of us was born.[29]

Looking at me quizzically, she asked: "Where you come from?" I wondered if I was extra-terrestrial, from Mars maybe. "Yah must come back and hold up he hand in prayer," she continued.

I had just left Ben's room. It was not my first visit. The elderly lady was part of Ben's domestic staff. I suspected that she was outside the room listening while I was talking and praying privately with Ben. My interesting encounter with Ben is outlined in one of the Prayer Letters. He passed less than a month after that visit.

The question is not so much where have I come from, but more where am I going. I subsequently reflected that I really am not of this world. My heart is not wired here. I am a pilgrim. No cliché!

---

[29] Lloyd John Oglivie, *Falling Into Greatness*, Thomas Nelson Publishers Copyright 1984. p 117

Lloyd John Oglivie in his book *Falling Into Greatness* expounds on Psalm 84 showing what being a pilgrim really means. For our pilgrimage, we will need a pilgrim's purpose, a pilgrim's heart and the pilgrim's power.

Very poignant is his exposition on the people (pilgrims) who passing through the Valley of Baca are able to make it a well. He intimates that:

> *Great people are those who, because their pilgrim purpose is to glorify God, can see the potential wrapped up in problems. They ask: What can I learn from this? What is the Lord seeking to teach me? What does He want me to dare to ask and expect?*[30]

He continues as he emphasizes that:

> *The greater our purpose, the greater our positive expectation of blessing. When we seek His will and His specific direction of what to pray, He gives us exactly what we need in the problems that confront us. We unwrap the problem, take it apart, grapple with it as a stepping stone to greater growth, and allow the Lord to show us His solution.*[31]

This exposition is on point. I certainly want to keep my pilgrim's heart. What about you?

****

---

[30] Ibid. p 123
[31] Ibid. p. 123

God's Superior Plan

———•❈•———

But he knows the way that I take; when he has tested me, I will come forth as gold. Job 23:10 NIV

For I know the plans I have for you, declares the LORD, plans to prosper you and not to harm you, plans to give you hope and a future. Jeremiah 29:11

It is very comforting to know and deeply believe that God knows the way we are taking. He knows our journey, which may also be a test. At times folk may think they understand our journey; they know the way we are taking. Such myopic thinking is reflected in such statements as: 'I know what you are going through.' Maybe, it is intended to be a statement of commiseration. Have you ever encountered such?

But really and truly *only God knows* and His knowledge is perfect and panoramic. He sees the day of our birth and the day of our departure and all the days in between – our dash, as it is called. With such perfect knowledge He can chart our course. If the process of alchemy takes us through a crucible experience, then we must emerge as pure gold, not fool's gold. (See 1 Peter 1: 6 & 7)

In 2003 when I realized that my health was changing, I told my church family not to pray for my healing but to pray that the will of God be done. I would *never* want anyone to tell God what to do with me. Why? It is God, *not man,* who wrote all my days in my book of life before I even lived one of them. (See Psalm 139) I trust God. I trust in the goodness of His character. I trust in His unfailing love. God must trust me too. I dare not disappoint Him!

****

Read His lips

My covenant will I not break, nor alter the thing that is gone out of my lips. Psalm 89:34

Wow, this is straight from the "horse's mouth" so to speak. Very succinctly, God tells us that He does not go back on His word. If there is any backtracking, it would have to be on our side. If God says that He will help you in any situation, and bring you through, then you have to stand on that word. Sometimes, the way out, has to be *through.*

The way to escape is that you *bear* it, not *escape* it. (See 1 Corinthians 10:13) Indeed, would we not want to hasten our escape from the storm? (Psalm 55:8) One writer says that we are good escape artists. We may be so busy trying to escape the storm that we do not even wait to listen to the One who can teach us how to weather the storm.

God describes Himself as having lips and speaking to us... so in essence, God is saying, "Read my lips." Most folk possibly spend more time reading their circumstances than reading God's lips and internalizing what He has said. God does not intend to be a divine ventriloquist. We read His lips by reading His promises which are not blurred and obscure...hence we need not stumble. Those who love your instructions have great peace and do not stumble. Psalm 119:165 (NLT)

****

Knowing God's Name

"If you'll hold on to me for dear life," says God, "I'll get you out of any trouble I'll give you the best of care if you'll only get to know and trust me. Call me and I'll answer, be at your side in bad times; I'll rescue you, then throw you a party. I'll give you a long life, give you a long drink of salvation!" Psalm 91:14 & 15 (The Message Bible)

These verses, rich with meaning and promises, also include conditions. The conditions, stated and inferred, are that such an individual whom God will bless magnanimously will love Him. This will not be a puppy, emotional type love but a love of the quality which is described in Deuteronomy 20:20. Such a person will turn to God for help and will receive it. The condition of our receiving help is that we must ask God. We would not seek His aid if we do not trust Him.

The clause "because he hath known my name" refers to an individual understanding God's character. God's name represents His character, so when we pollute His name, however we do it, we are besmirching His character. Once we have truly tasted (experienced) and seen that God is good, we will automatically love Him.

We will not be held in bondage to the various caricatures of God which abound, and prevent us from trusting Him as it is our privilege to do. Some of those distorted views of God include seeing Him as being a vengeful and angry judge, watching over us to catch us out in our mistakes and promptly punishing us.

I never doubted the existence of God, but for me He was an absentee God. He was not a Father who wanted an intimate Father/daughter relationship with me. I was afraid of God until...I actually met Him. God gave Moses a picture of Himself. We must believe what He says about His character. (See Exodus 33:19) Knowing God's name will impact on how we respond to the tests and trials of life. God makes it clear what He will do for those who know His name. We simply have to believe that He is a 'Man of His word'!

****

Chased Down and Rescued by Mercy

---·◈·---

*Surely goodness and mercy shall follow me all
the days of my life. Psalm 23:6*

In the very depths of your heart, are you convinced beyond
the shadow of a thread of doubt that God really loves you?
He certainly does! Sometimes things may change in our life,
and outwardly, it looks as if it will be our 'undoing'. However,
inwardly, we know that God is doing an 'awesome thing'? Has
that ever happened to you? In my journey with God, I have
always felt very much loved and even honoured that God could
trust me not to pollute His name. (See Psalm 115:2)

For some people, a change in life's circumstances can bring to
the surface deep hidden feelings about God and His mercy.
How did those feelings get there in the first place? The adults
and significant others in our lives would have influenced our
subconscious feelings about God. For some people, those hidden
feelings about God would need to be healed and changed. An
excellent book to read on that issue would be a book called
Redeeming the Past by David A. Seamands.

Many folk will begin to question whether God really loves them
when tests or trials come. Not only question, but sometimes
outright rebel and vehemently castigate God. Or, of an even more
insidious nature, quietly seethe in anger, while going through

the motions of submitting to the will of God. The immediate assumption is that God is punishing them.

In the 'old time days' as we say in Bajan parlance, some parents in administering corporal punishment, with their chosen instrument, would synchronise their words of chastisement with their strokes. With each descending blow, it would be said with much emphasis: "I, (whack) punishing you (whack) for your good." (whack) The whacks were not silent either. Just imagine if the parent had a lot to say...

Those days, hopefully are over. I never personally experienced any such treatment because my Mum was more of a talker and I was not a recalcitrant child, not perfect by any means, but not a 'trouble tree'.

More than we might realise, we can transfer how we feel about our parents to how we feel about God. They punished us for our good and so God must do the same. There is however a chasm between how humans would punish and how God chastises, which is more a correction, designed to save our very lives, and never applied in any vindictive, vehement or cruel manner. I was shocked to hear a gentleman at the gym talk about his days of punishment. 'Jack' said His dad would soak a dog hunter in water and beat him, after the beating salt water would be thrown on him. Goodness! That is unconscionable child abuse!!

If someone had experiences with parents (or even teachers) where punishment was administered in ways which caused that individual to feel abused in some form or fashion, it can impact on that individual's later relationship with God. Seamands in his book 'Redeeming the Past' explores that idea and it is a book worth your reading.

So when life changes in an apparently negative way for some folk, they will begin to feel that God is no longer merciful. Suddenly

His character has changed. No, God never changes in His love toward us. Never! He is not a 'Jekyll and Hyde' character. The Apostle Paul experienced the love of God in such a deep way that He proclaims the unchangeable nature of that love in clarion tones in Romans Chapter 8.

If we are able to place every single thing that comes into our lives into the melting pot of God's love, we would have to declare with the Apostle that *nothing* can separate us from that love and that indeed in *all these things*, we can be more than conquerors. I think that anything I may be called upon to go through would be mere peanuts compared to what the Apostle Paul endured.

I have experienced God's mercy in such incredible ways. On December 7, 2013, I shared with the Belleplaine Church family on the theme of taking responsibility for your health. I noted that December 1st was the tenth anniversary of what I call *The Intruder Incident*. This divinely orchestrated incident carried a strong proleptic message. Here I am ten years after that time referring to it. God has been merciful to me.

The Bible talks about the fear of the Lord and the fear of the Lord contributes to longevity. This fear of the Lord involves respecting Him and what He says. It also involves respecting His laws, both the moral law and the laws of nature and those laws that govern the functioning of our bodies.

It is always God's intent to be merciful to us. In mercy, He does not always immediately extricate us from our difficulties but He shows us how to get *through* them. In this way, we actually experience or *taste* of the mercies of God. O taste and see that God is good!!

He declares Himself to be a merciful God and that mercy chases us down, even to the very last day of our lives on this earth.

Surely goodness and mercy shall follow me *all the days of my life*. God's opens up His umbrella of mercy over us and we are privileged to be always under its shade. Are you basking under your umbrella? I sure hope that you are!

****

Reaping What You Have Sown

---·◈·---

God hath spoken once, twice have I heard this; that power belongeth unto God. Also unto thee, O Lord, belongeth mercy: for thou renderest to every man according to His work. Psalm 62:11

Don't be misled: No one makes a fool of God. What a person plants, he will harvest. The person who plants selfishness, ignoring the needs of others—ignoring God!—harvests a crop of weeds. All he'll have to show for his life is weeds! But the one who plants in response to God, letting God's Spirit do the growth work in him, harvests a crop of real life, eternal life. Galatians 6:7 & 8 (Message Bible)

What we sow, we will reap, is generally understood in a negative light. However, the spiritual principle embedded in this text can work very positively where we have been sowing to the spirit. We sow to the spirit when we invest time in building and strengthening our relationship with God over the years.

Elizabeth George in her book: "A Woman after God's Own Heart", makes the point that we may be tempted to think that quiet hidden time with God does not count. No one sees us over the years as we spend quiet time with God; no one sees us meditating on and memorizing God's Word. God alone sees.

However, we are quietly building strength. I recollect that I shared a message at The Maranatha SDA church in 2002, which was aired on one of our radio stations. The title of the message was the same as the book.

We cannot have been sowing to the flesh and then expect to reap the fruit of Spirit. The storms of life will reveal where we have been sowing. Peace, joy and faith will be rendered to us, *according to our work*. An interesting aspect of the sowing and reaping principle is that while sowing can be done unobtrusively, what is reaped is clearly seen. The poem: *The Seasons of My Life* creatively captures my reflection of my growth with God.

The Seasons of My Life

Summer has gone
You walked with me then
In the sunshine and glow of youth
At 23 we locked hands...
But before that
You seemed so distant, so cold, so aloof
I did not know you
Felt I had grieved you in some way
Maybe you had just left
But on that memorable night
You exploded into my life and
Washed me with torrents of rain
Suddenly, Your love became so real
I felt so excited
I wondered if others had met you in the same way
I'd look into eyes to see if I could detect...
That excitement was not like the fake one
I had learnt how to conjure up

In passionate but hollow 'prayerless' prayers
We met early in the mornings
Always a refreshing time
Sometimes crying, sometimes laughing.
Many times in deep contemplation of your love
I wept, deep sobs...
As you led me through 'The Desire of Ages"
Showing me Yourself
A time of reflection, meditation and introspection
No one to shout: 'Mummy!'
Time was mine to submerge myself as long as I cared to
And I cared.....
We courted quietly beside the still streams
Weeks turned into months
Months changed to years
As I quietly grew in the shade
and warmth of your succulent love
Feasting on the nectar of your Word
Watered by the gentle sprinklings of Your Holy Spirit
Like a gentle flower
My petals started to unfold
Like a fruit ripening in the warmth of the sun
You sent the rain to ripen me
You never pick a fruit before its time
Now in the autumn of my life
You have brought spring
A God of the impossible
Spring in Autumn
You beautify me with the colours of your love
'Seasons of mists and mellow fruitfulness'
You did promise that I would
Walk through this season well watered
Lacking nothing.....nothing!!
What a God!
Your pruning has made my growth luxuriant
The most beautiful season of my life

A season of maturity
In the scheme of things winter follows autumn
But He who turned back the clock dial as a sign
Can again turn back winter
And bring spring
A season of colour, life and rejuvenation
Yes, indeed God can make any season one.....
of mellow fruitfulness.

Comment: God sends rain into our lives, not to drown us, but to ripen us for His eternal purposes. When it rains, let's be the rainbow in the rain.

Nola Estwick

Composed February 2006

****

God the Perfect Connoisseur

—————•◉•—————

And we know that all things work together for good to them that love God, to them who are the called according to his purpose. Romans 8:28

All aspects of a person's life's journey may not appear to be 'good'. Words like 'good' and 'bad', 'negative' and 'positive' become relative when we are walking with God. Often, our 'bad' is actually God's 'good'. Our 'setback' is often God's setup... as strategically designed.

The above text is often truncated to say 'all things work together for good'. But that is not the case! The most critical part of the text is *'to them that love God'*. For indeed, if you love God for Himself and not simply for His blessings, then His love will lead you to see the bigger picture and not simply the specific testing circumstance before you.

The outworking all depends on your response. I have seen in my life's experiences the marvellous 'working together for good' about which this text speaks. It has been totally awesome! I have shared many, many goodies in those letters before I turned off the faucet in 2010. There is still more in the pipeline!

My dear friend, mentor and former teacher, the late Ruby St. John, who was one of my main proof-readers for the manuscript with the Prayer Letters, often commented on the force of the letters. On more than one occasion Ruby would say: "Nola, that blew me away." Or she'd say: 'I would give you an 'A' for that letter.' Ruby was indeed a positive and encouraging person!

Without a doubt, God's purpose towards me has always been one of benevolent kindness. Maybe onlookers felt that I would die of thirst at 'Marah' but God knew how He would replenish me.

****

What Soothsayers Don't Know About Saying

—•❈•—

Have faith in God, Jesus answered. Truly I tell you, if anyone says to this mountain, 'Go, throw yourself into the sea,' and does not doubt in their heart but believes that what they say will happen, it will be done for them. Therefore I tell you, whatever you ask for in prayer, believe that you have received it, and it will be yours. **Mark 11:22-24 NIV**

According to the dictionary a soothsayer is a person who predicts the future by magical, intuitive, or more rational means: prognosticator. Can there be soothsayers in our lives? Of course! They are people who usually predict, but their predictions tend to be negative, though not always. Using their metaphorical crystal balls, tarot cards or their palm reading skills, they foretell our future. Of course, *they never use the Bible* and may have a mere passing knowledge *or no knowledge at all* of Jeremiah 28:11. Soothsayers are not acquainted with Lamentations 3:37.

The divine principles embedded in the above texts may be totally foreign to those on the soothsaying bandwagon; or they may misapply the principles. It is important to understand that Jesus spoke the words in Mark 11:22-24 to *His disciples, not to Tom, Dick and Harry*. Divine principles can be misconstrued by those who are about pushing their agenda and following their own will.

The text reiterates the word *say*. It is one thing to believe, but speaking is equally important. What you *say* with your mouth should synchronise with what you believe in your heart. In the spiritual realm, there should be no dichotomy.

Speaking the word *God has given you* is what is critical, *not what you made up and gave yourself.* To avoid a misapplication of this text, it would be wisdom to ask whether what you are speaking is what God *has already spoken,* that is, what He has already decreed. Nothing shall be impossible to us as long as it is *in the will of God for us.*

I cannot help but reflect on a situation where an individual was very ill. Some folk loudly declared that he would be restored and they *said* with great assurance what would happen. He would live and would accomplish 'this and that'. I must admit when I heard the loud declarations, I wondered if it was a case of trying to bulldoze God under the guise of 'speaking to the mountain'.

Irony of ironies, when the sick individual finally spoke, would you believe that *he* immediately said that we have to submit to the will of Almighty God? Admirably calm and cool he was. His attitude was the complete opposite of those, who though wanting him to recuperate, did not consider God's will. How was it eventually resolved? Well, he died. *Those positive declarations were man's will and not God's.*

So does that rule out being positive and speaking positively? Not at all! However, God is not our 'yard boy' for us, under the guise of 'faith' to dictate to Him what He must do. I hold very strongly with the advice given with respect to praying for the sick which is found in the book *The Ministry of Healing*. This is sane, sensible and sound instruction! Please read the entire chapter entitled *Prayer For The Sick.*

> *God knows the end from the beginning. He is acquainted with the hearts of all men. He reads every secret of the soul. He knows whether those for whom prayer is offered would or would not be able to endure the trials that would come upon them should they live. He knows whether their lives would be a blessing or a curse to themselves and to the world. This is one reason why, while presenting our petitions with earnestness, we should say, "Nevertheless not my will, but Thine, be done. Luke 22:42*

> *The consistent course is to commit our desires to our all-wise heavenly Father, and then, in perfect confidence, trust all to Him. We know that God hears us if we ask according to His will. But to press our petitions without a submissive spirit is not right; our prayers must take the form, not of command, but of intercession.* (My italics)[32]

We can all 'soothsay', be it good or bad, but it really does boil down to whether God gave a word. The story of the centurion's servant found in the book of Matthew demonstrates a person who understood the principle of speaking the Word of God in faith! (Read the narrative in Matthew 8.) In response to his marvellous faith when he said to Jesus "...speak the word only, and my servant shall be healed." (Verse 8) Jesus gave him in a word when He told the man: "Go! Let it be done just as you believed it would." NIV (Verse 13)

---

[32] Ellen G. White, *Ministry of Healing,* Pacific Press Publishing Association, Mountain View, California (1905) p. 230

The centurion left with no other evidence to stand on but the Word of Jesus. On his way home, if someone had asked him, "How is your servant doing?" What do you imagined he might have said? 'I gaw go and see if he dead yet.' (Standard English: I have to go and see whether he has died as yet.) Or, based on what Jesus, the Healer, had told him, might he have spoken positively?

The Biblical narrative tells us that the centurion was met on the way and he learnt that the very hour Jesus had spoken to him, was in fact the very hour his servant was healed. But you may argue that the centurion was not a disciple. Faith is not tied to a church pew; it exists in the hearts of people. There is of course a mocking irony in this story.

God knows those who genuinely trust in Him. (See Nahum 1:7) Being very positive and speaking positively, underneath the umbrella of God's will, is not denial disguised, but represents an unfaltering faith, which is securely fastened to the infallible Word of God.

There is saying and there is *saying – God's saying.* Romans 9:15 indicates that God will have mercy on whom He will, that is His prerogative. He says to Moses, "I will have mercy on whom I have mercy, and I will have compassion on whom I have compassion." (See Exodus 33:19)

I discovered this thought provoking text a long time ago: "Who can speak and have it happen if the Lord has not decreed it?" Lamentations 3:37 NIV

When all the 'sayers' have wearied themselves out with their predictions and prognostications, *God always has the last say!*

****

Bitter Waters Turned Sweet

---·◉·---

Now when they came to Marah, they could not drink the waters of Marah, for they were bitter. Therefore the name of it was called Marah. And the people complained against Moses, saying, 'What shall we drink?' So he cried out to the LORD, and the LORD showed him a tree. When he cast it into the waters, the waters were made sweet. Exodus 15: 23-25 NKJV

Life will have its metaphorical 'Marahs'. You may be familiar with the following story. The Israelites had been journeying for a number of days and were very thirsty. Coming upon this place with water, they were no doubt elated. But alas, the waters were bitter and so we have the name Marah, meaning bitter. The Israelites did what most of us would be inclined to do. They grumbled and fretted and became furious with Moses.

What happens when we come to the 'Marahs' in our life's journey – those testing situations which have the potential for making us either bitter or better? We can choose to fret and grumble, forgetting God's past mercies, or like Moses, we can cry out to God for His aid. He never fails. With His impeccable foresight, God already had a solution in place. He showed Moses a piece of wood which Moses promptly threw into the water. Immediately the water was made sweet and the Israelites were able to drink it.

Can sweet come out of bitter? As I relate this scenario to my situation, I have always felt that what you name a thing, that is exactly how it will be to you. It's not any psychological gimmickry, it is a life principle. (See Job 22:28) I have always labelled my experience as an adventure with God. That's how I see it; that is how I have lived my journey. There has never been a "Why me?" Cynicism, bitterness, questioning, repining have never, for one moment, reared their ugly heads in my life. In fact, could we say: 'Why *not* me?' The main publication outlines several of my adventurous encounters with people.

Marah was where God proved His people. God will prove us as well with testing situations. One thing is certain: He will never give us more than we can bear and He weighs each test. My Pastor recently postulated that a major test represents God's vote of confidence in you. As it were God says: 'You can handle it.' And Pastor Joseph is correct. God does not give us tests to sit back and watch us flounder and fail. Not at all! Depending on His power, we can ace the tests of life.

God can teach us how to handle our Marahs with divine grace, poise and dignity. From Marah, God led His people to Elim, a place which had twelve springs and seventy palm trees. What is the lesson for us? Whatever experiences we meet in life that appear to be against us, we can count on God, the greatest alchemist ever, to transform them and redeem them for our good, and indeed the good of others.

He is also the perfect connoisseur and can take the 'lemons' of our lives and make the best lemonade ever!! Want some??

****

Decree God's decree

———————•❖•———————

Death and life are in the power of the tongue.
Proverbs 18:21

Thou shalt also decree a thing, and it shall
be established unto thee: and the light shall
shine upon thy ways. Job 22:28

Job 22:28 is also rendered: You will decide
on a matter, and it will be established for
you, and light will shine on your ways. (ESV
Translation)

The spiritual laws and principles embedded in these texts may
well be missed. Our words help to create our destiny and in that
sense death and life are in the power of the tongue. How can
we declare something and it be established unto us? We have to
decree what *God* has directed us to decree. It would be unwise
to 'up' (to use Bajan parlance) and start decreeing wild, without
consulting the will of God. For example, God decreed that He
had given the land to the Israelites, when the twelve spies had
gone to check out their new territory. Yet, only two of the spies
declared what God had told them.

They spoke very positively and said that with God on their side
they could be very successful. However, the ten spies allowed
what they could *see* to overwhelm them and declared that they

110

could not conquer the land. God had already said that He *had given* them the land – a divine fiat! We can stand on that.

Regrettably, the ten spies reaped the fruit of their words. They never entered the Promised Land. However, Joshua and Caleb did! Our words do create our destiny!

An excellent book for you to read would be the book: 'The Power of Your Words' by Gosset and Trent. Also very instructive would be John Ortberg's book: If You Want to Walk on Water, You Have to Get Out of the Boat.

****

Nourished in the Desert

---◦❖◦---

The LORD will guide you always; he will satisfy your needs in a sun-scorched land and will strengthen your frame. You will be like a well-watered garden, like a spring whose waters never fail. Isaiah 58:11 (NIV translation)

Streams of living water will flow from deep within the person who believes in me. John 7:38 (God's Word Translation)

I love the imagery in Isaiah 58:11 and its underlying meaning. To have your needs satisfied in a sun-scorched land is like being nourished in the desert. In a place where nourishment is least expected, God supplies all that is needed. In my journey with God over the last nine years in particular, God has surely strengthened my frame. It's a slender frame but it sure is strong. All of my needs have been met... all!

It is important to remember that we are not speaking about physical places since this is all imagery. This is symbolic of spiritual positions, where we can be in Christ. To be like a well-watered garden in a sun scorched place is therefore a state of being which is supernaturally bestowed. The idea conveyed is that even in 'desert' experiences we will be nourished and will give nourishment to others.

John 7:38 also picks up the water imagery and extends the meaning of the metaphor. The water comes from deep within the person, or from the belly. The belly, as opposed to the mouth, is significant. From the mouth can come things which we have not experienced. Sharing from your "guts", your deep experiences, speaks to being thoroughly authentic, no mere fluff! People are smart, they can read us! Gut experiences can be effective in influencing people for the Kingdom of God.

****

A Fine Stallion

———————————•❖•———————————

And they thirsted not when he led them through the deserts: he caused the waters to flow out of the rock for them: he clave the rock also, and the waters gushed out. Isaiah 48:21 ASV

Where is the one who led them through the bottom of the sea? They were like fine stallions racing through the desert, never stumbling. Isaiah 63:13 (NLT)

When we are on any journey with God, when we have His presence, our souls will dwell at ease and we will be peaceful. A journey embarked on alone, will result in misery, fretfulness, stress, frustration and a spirit heavier than a sand bag. My journey has not 'dried' me out.

God has truly provided for every single one of my needs. In fact, those closest to me, my family, who see me every day, have never seen me acting in any way to cause them alarm. Neither have they ever heard me utter a single word which has caused them to feel any trepidation for me.

I have never left household duties undone because I was not well, never missed school or church because I was terribly ill and laid up. Sheer tiredness at times demanded some 'time out'. My day always begins between four and five, at times even earlier. My trips to the gym were never once curtailed because of 'illness'. Colds and the flu were minimal to almost non-existent.

Each year, excluding last year, I have travelled extensively, enjoying two long leaves, travelling alone to England and to several American States. At one point I travelled by bus from New York way over to Florida, making several stops as I visited friends and family along the way. God was indeed an excellent travelling Companion. As I shared evidence of smooth sailing on my journey with 'Jane' recently, she appeared shocked. Maybe, she is not alone.

God has given to me so magnanimously during this time that I have been able to give to others. From 2003 until this time, there has never been a Friday evening that I was unable to prepare Sabbath lunch. We have friends coming to share lunch with us practically every Sabbath. This hospitality ministry has not ceased. Many people have given to me during this time as well, in a variety of ways, too numerous to mention! Were I to breathe even one word of complaint, *I would be an utterly ungrateful, mean-spirited wretch.* I have no choice but to be an overflowing reservoir of gratitude!

****

Real 'Nuff' Grace

Each time he said, My grace is all you need. My power works best in weakness. So now I am glad to boast about my weaknesses, so that the power of Christ can work through me. (NLT) Other translations say: "...so that the power of Christ can rest on me or dwell in me." 2 Corinthians 12:9 NLT

I am blown away by the idea of God's grace, not to mention experiencing what it means to walk in that grace – undeserved favour. God's grace encompasses His kindness, mercy, longsuffering, tenderness, compassion and sensitivity, among His other attributes. He tells us that all we need is His grace. It is sufficient. What a perfect example of litotes. This is a literary device we understate a situation, not painting it to be as strong or intense as it really is. To me, God's grace is not merely sufficient; it is super abundant, copious beyond measure and constantly overflowing. Such grace is magnanimously bestowed on us. Really, what more could we ask for?

Here's a snippet from the Prayer Letter entitled Sufficient Grace written in June 2006:

God's grace and power are mountainous to those who honour Him by showing that they trust Him before they trust 'the sons of men'." (Psalm

31:19) Does the Word not say that if we have faith enough we could say to this mountain be removed? (Matthew 17:20)

Hey, you mountain, just get out of my way and let me pass!! No, not quite like that! (LOL) Here is an interesting comment from one of my favourite writers:

Faith takes God at His Word, not asking to understand the meaning of the trying experiences that come. But there are <u>many</u> who have <u>little faith</u>.[33]

God's grace being sufficient means that I will lack nothing. I can be more than a conqueror. The sufficiency is not in me but it is entirely in God!!!

Not that we are sufficient of ourselves to think anything as of ourselves: but our sufficiency is of God. 2 Corinthians 3:5 [34]End of quoted extract.)

Finally, a paradox which is evident from this text is that when we are weakest, that is the very time we are the strongest. To be weak and strong at the same time is, logically speaking, incongruous. But in the spiritual realm incongruities can be the norm!

So as I further noted in the prayer letter:

When I am asked: 'How are you doing?' I love to preface my answer with the statement: 'By the grace of God'. Now that is by no means a glib cliché response. The term by the grace of God taken to its full depth of meaning is very powerful!! With that

---

[33] Ellen G. White, *Promises for The Last Days*, Review and Herald Publishing Association, Washington, DC 20039 (1994) p. 63

[34] Prayer Letter entitled Sufficient Grace written in June 2006

*as an introductory phrase, I then cannot add such
lame appendages as: 'I hey', 'I surviving', 'I en too
bad' 'I half hearty' 'I okay' or 'I could be worse'.
I must say: 'I am excellent, superb, and absolutely
wonderful! Marvellous!'*

*A little naughty as I can get sometimes, I love to
observe the reaction of persons who may think that I
am 'on my last leg out' when I respond so positively.
Yes, if there is any denial, it would have to be that
we are in denial of the power of God!* [35](End of
quoted extract)

So, how am I doing? I am magnificently blessed! That tune, by
God's grace, needs never change. (See Job 21:23-25) 'Brandon's'
(one of my valley connections) very last words, hoarsely
whispered, to me were: "Praise God!" He lived a 'praise God
life' and died a 'praise God death'! Have you ever thought what
you would like your last words to be?

****

---

[35] Ibid

Fire Proof

---•◉•---

When thou passest through the waters, I will be with thee; and through the rivers, they shall not overflow thee: when thou walkest through the fire, thou shalt not be burned; neither shall the flame kindle upon thee. Isaiah 43:2

This message or promise from God is one of my strongest assurances of how God's power may be manifested in my life. This text tells us exactly what God will do when we pass through rivers, water and fire and what the result will be. The imagery refers to various levels of tests, trials and difficulties. These things do not scare God because He is above them. I smiled to myself when I read that God sits upon the flood. (Psalm 29:10) I noted also that God chose to have His people go through the flood *on foot.* (Psalm 66:6)

It is not a matter of if but *when* we experience any kind of trial. The apostle Peter cautions us as he says: "Dear friends, do not be surprised at the fiery ordeal that has come on you to test you, as though something strange were happening to you." (1 Peter 4:12 NIV) Some Christians are shocked when they are tested in unexpected ways because they have misguided notions about the Christian life. Some may be excited about starting a 'ministry' but they want one that costs them nothing. We are more compassionate 'ministers' when we have gone through some trying experience and can empathize.

God will indeed take us through. His promises are there to fully sustain us, so that we are not incinerated or drowned by the experience. Inside we can be calm, peaceful and thoroughly at rest, fully confident and trusting in the impeccable care of God. Once we have divinely tutored in the crucible, then we are qualified to help others through their times, and not simply throw glib empty cliché phrases at them.

I learnt in my reading just recently that in the centre of the flame there is a hollow. Did you know that? That scientific fact was proved via an experiment. The spiritual application which the writer then drew was that once we are in the hollow of the flame, we will not be burnt. It is when we become agitated and shift about that the flames can hurt us. To be in a fiery experience and feel no heat is indeed a supernatural experience. Fiery experiences will come, for by them God works to purify us. We can walk around in the fire, knowing there will be a "fourth man" with us. (See Daniel 3: 24 & 25)

****

In Peace... Not Pieces!

Do not be anxious about anything, but in every situation, by prayer and petition, with thanksgiving, present your requests to God. [7] And the peace of God, which transcends all understanding, will guard your hearts and your minds in Christ Jesus. Philippians 4: 6 & 7 NIV

Could this be any clearer? The formula for peace is right here! Then why do so many of us as Christians fret and worry ourselves to a frazzle? We talk about pray and committing a situation to God and then still turn around and worry and fret. We even sing with gusto: *O what peace we often forfeit, O what needless pain we bear, All because we do not carry everything to God in prayer.* Then, we live what we have sung!

The word 'forfeit' means to: "to lose or lose the right to, especially by some error, offense, or crime. "The peace we forfeit was by rights ours. We had it or had access to it but gave it up. We gave up the right to it. By His life and death Jesus purchased peace for us. The enemy cannot snatch peace from us; we would have to relinquish it. Jesus would not issue an impossible command. If He tells us not to be anxious about anything, it means He can achieve that in us, not that we can do it in ourselves.

I respectfully listen to, but will never argue with those Christians who say that you must worry: "Yeah, yuh is only human so yah got to worry."[36] Though they do not realize it, they are actually undermining the power of God's Word. We excuse our inability to walk in the power of God's Word because we use our carnal nature as a scapegoat.

It would be better to just admit our tendency to worry and acknowledge that God is still working on us, and will help us to overcome, as we grow to trust Him more and more. It's certainly not an overnight thing. Someday we will surprise ourselves that we can walk in complete peace and calm in a testing situation, when previously, we would have fallen apart.

Acknowledging a weakness is *much better* than saying that we cannot be delivered from worry. When you say something cannot happen, when God Himself says it is possible, it just means that it will never happen *to you*! Such naysayers will be snared by the very words of their mouths.

To connect this text to my journey, I can truthfully say that God totally calmed me. My family has never been in any panic about me. They have all recorded their comments in the letter *Input From Others*. They have seen me change my lifestyle and they have seen me going to the gym. Of course, they have heard some of the various presentations I have made. God has blessed our entire family with peace.

God promises us to keep us in peace if our thoughts are stayed or focussed on Him. Positive thoughts are pivotal to our wellbeing. In an article published in our local newspaper, The Nation, I addressed the issue of positive thoughts. See appendix. My husband Andy, has been a very positive and supportive person

---

[36] Bajan dialect (dialect of Barbadians)

indeed. He has played his role excellently as a real 'helpmeet' and not simply a 'help me eat'!!

That peace, assurance and tranquillity with which God has so copiously blessed me, I have passed on to my family. My children know that their Mum is not "putting up a front". God makes His intention clear in Proverbs 3:33: The LORD curses the house of wicked people, but He blesses the home of righteous people. God's blessing is also felt as He carries us. You cannot carry someone from a distance; it has to be a close-up experience – one of deepest intimacy, where you see, feel and even smell the goodness of God!

****

Carried in Style

——— ·❖· ———

Hearken unto me, O house of Jacob, and all
the remnant of the house of Israel, which are
borne by me from the belly, which are carried
from the womb: Isaiah 46:3 & 4

The eternal God is thy refuge, and underneath
are the everlasting arms. Deuteronomy 33:27

Most of us are familiar with the poem called *Footprints in The Sand*. Apparently there has been a battle over its true author. (See sites: http://www.ruthshaven.com/christian/footprints. html and http://www.nydailynews.com/entertainment/ music-arts/3-way-battle-footprints-poem-article-1.328223.

I was led to believe that the persona was a man. But it seems to be a woman. It is ironic that the time she felt deserted, as she was only seeing one set of footprints, was the very time that the Lord was actually carrying her. What if the persona had known this *while on her journey* rather than at the end? It certainly would have made a difference to how she travelled.

In 2003, one of my dear spiritual friends gave me a plaque with 'Footprints in The Sand' and told me in no uncertain terms that God would *carry* me. I remember that day so well as Joanna stood in the 'South' staffroom of our school and gave me that profound 'proleptic' message. Pastor Joanna Charles-Greaves is the same friend who delivered a divinely inspired letter to me in January 2004.

God has strong enough arms to carry His children through anything. Some people go through very rough situations: family trauma, separation, divorce, abuse and such like, and were it not for God carrying them, as they trusted in Him, they would shackle apart. Others are confronted with changes in their health, financial circumstances, or traumatic changes in relationships with others, but they make it through. They survive.

But some folk may be so weather-beaten as they are buffeted by the winds of adversity, that they lose the joy of living. But it is not just to *scrape through* our tests. God wants us to valiantly make it through, with a testimony in our hearts and lives, having experienced that indeed underneath are/were the 'Everlasting Arms'.

To know that God is carrying you, not cosmetically, but in reality, makes a decided difference in how you respond to all of the vicissitudes of life. God promises that He would *never* leave nor forsake us, but if that is not sufficient, He says He will carry us. He never makes empty promises. He can, and does, come through on His word. His arm is certainly not short. (See Numbers 11:23)

If we want to be carried by God then we would have to be *in His arms*. It is a choice to be there and stay there. The Bible says that time and chance happens to every man, (see Ecclesiastes 9:11) so there will be a time for each of us to prove the validity of God's promises. When such a time comes, remember the texts quoted above and choose to ride hobby class! And, if you are riding hobby class, you cannot then, be falling to pieces.

****

A Mind Stayed on God

————————•◦❂◦•————————

Thou wilt keep him in perfect peace, whose mind is stayed on thee: because he trusteth in thee. Trust ye in the LORD forever: for in the LORD JEHOVAH is everlasting strength: Isaiah 26:3

A strong connective text to Philippians 4:6 & 7 is Isaiah 26:3. In this divine promise God says that *He will keep us*. It is His responsibility to do so. Our part is to let Him do it. If only we could let God be God! Our part is to keep our minds stayed on Him, not on the problem. The naysayers who try to keep themselves will be woefully defeated each time. Hence, they will think it is impossible. Once we understand the secret in Psalm 91:1, we are set for life!!!

This peace of God which is an antidote to worry is supernaturally bestowed. It emanates from living life in the Spirit. The flesh is absolutely powerless to generate genuine peace. You simply cannot fake this peace. Possibly, for a day or a week, you could put up a good show, a nice façade. But to achieve this feat for years is highly unlikely, if not totally impossible!! If you are walking in the Spirit and not in the flesh, you *must be* peaceful. There is simply no argument. Through the power of the Spirit you can walk in peace and not fall to pieces!

This supernatural peace is an enigma to the carnal man. The Bible says that he cannot understand the things of the spirit. They are foolishness to him. (See 1 Corinthians 2:14) What you see depends on the lens you are looking at life through. What you see becomes your reality.

Persons looking through lens coloured by an earthly perspective will see things differently. Observing the Christian during his stormy times, and they have a right to do so, they will be looking to see evidence of this 'trust in God' which we as Christians claim to have. When they see us faltering, behaving as if we have no Heavenly Father to care for our needs, they are led to sneeringly and mockingly ask: 'Where now is their God?' (See Psalm 115:2) Or they may sarcastically say, as I Bajanise it: "Wuh I thought she/he did a Christian, wid all de big talk bout God and ting, wuh happen now? 'Huh, duh God mussee dead."[37]

Thus, unwittingly so, we cast aspersions on the character of God because we make Him out to be impotent. We do not show that He has the power to keep and carry His child. But suffused by the peace of God, we can confidently show them: Our God *is in the Heavens!! (Psalm 115:3)* He is not impotent but *omnipotent*. Whatever He does is *always* well done. His children know that! Arguing with skeptics, the overt ones and the closet ones, will be of no avail. Showing is always better than telling!

****

---

[37] Bajan dialect (Barbadian diaect)

Experience – Life's Best Teacher

———◆———

*Before I was afflicted I went astray, but now
I obey your word. Psalm 119:67*

*For he does not willingly bring affliction or
grief to the children of men. Lamentations
3:33 NIV*

*It was good for me to be afflicted so that I
might learn your decrees. The law from your
mouth is more precious to me than thousands
of pieces of silver and gold. Psalm 119:71 NIV*

Perception affects response. The word affliction may conjure up negative connotations for many persons. Why me? We think of hardship and punishment. But we need to refocus and think of learning opportunities and growth. Depending on your response, your 'affliction" or blessing in disguise, can become what is known as a 'teachable moment'. The term 'the teachable moment' could be attributed to that period of your life's experience which is most propitious to your learning something that may not have been learnt otherwise.

Since response is the key to blessing, God offers free professional counseling. We would save ourselves a lot of money if we would check out God *first*. Proverbs 3:11 tells us not to despise the chastening of the Lord, neither be weary of his correction. Job reminds us that 'blessed is the man whom God corrects' (Job 5:17) and in Hebrews 12:5 & 6 we are admonished to take the Lord's rebuke or discipline seriously and not to "get an attitude". But alas, some of us as Christians do 'get an attitude'. A rebellious, negative and miserable attitude does not foster learning. We cannot be taught if we are busy throwing pity parties and licking our wounds.

What I have learnt in the realm of faith and of health has been so life changing that I am eternally grateful to God. I owe Him big time!! I must admit that being a Seventh-day Adventist placed me in an advantageous position where life changing and life enhancing information was at my disposal.

Information is power; it is life! I am fully aware that it is about being *in Christ* and not simply being *in a church*. However, there is a deep and indelible conviction that I could *not* have walked through my divinely ordained experience in the way that I have, had I not been exposed to the information on health which saturates the SDA church, as well as what real true trusting faith is all about, as outlined in the Spirit of Prophecy and all the other great literature on the life of faith. Talk about resources!!

Recently, Clinical Professor of Preventive Medicine, at Loma Linda University in California, Dr Hans Diehl, was in Barbados presenting critical information on health issues. The Barbados Drug Service sponsored a public lecture at the Lloyd Erskine Sandiford Centre.

I had heard Dr. Diehl several times before as he lectured at various SDA churches, but I still attended the lecture. I was thrilled to see Barbadians turn out in droves to hear Dr. Diehl speak on the topic: *The Prevention and Reversal of Chronic Illnesses in Barbados.* The auditorium was packed to capacity! Our Chief Medical Officer, Dr. Joy St. John was there and thanked him at the end for an excellent lecture. Sensitively educating people and encouraging them to make better choices is certainly the way of wisdom.

I am on the same page with Dr. Diehl. I have been blessed in knowing how to improve my eating habits. As they say, 'Necessity is the mother of invention'. I have learnt how to prepare very tasty totally vegan dishes, some of them are one hundred percent raw. I know how to sprout. So I can have my mung beans, lentils, garbanzos and other peas, sprouted and bursting with enzymes. Many foods which we feel we have to cook till they are totally dead, I can use raw. When I sit to eat, my plate looks like a rainbow of colours.

Trying to eat healthier meals and avoiding what tastes good but is a grave digger will not occur overnight. Our culture leads us to enjoy what is sweet, salty and greasy. We do have a perverted appetite with which to contend. But, there is hope for all of us! With the high rate of chronic diseases in Barbados, many people are ready to wake up and listen and not wait until they are forced to change. The phenomenal turn out to Dr. Diehl's lecture spoke volumes.

It has been my delight to take up opportunities to share health information interwoven with my personal experience. I have done this with many SDA church families, as well as sharing with several of my Christian brothers and sisters in other churches. The response, especially of my non SDA Christian friends, has always been very warm and overwhelmingly enthusiastic. So I have to say in the words of Psalmist: "It was good for me to be afflicted so that I might learn your decrees. The law from your mouth is more precious to me than thousands of pieces of silver and gold."

Cancel all your pity parties. Plan a praise party. So, rethink "affliction". It may well be your "blessing in disguise"!

****

'Affliction' Turned Blessing

---◆❀◆---

For you, O LORD, have made me glad by your work at the works of your hands I sing for joy. How great are your works, O LORD! Your thoughts are very deep! The stupid man cannot know; the fool cannot understand this: Psalm 92:4-6 ESV

The folly and stupidity referred to in this text have nothing to do with intellectual attainment or mental acumen. Intellectually sharp people can actually be very spiritually dull. The *fool* has said in his heart that there is no God.

These verses refer to those who are unable to comprehend things in the spiritual realm. They are unable to grasp the works of God. They can only see and interpret things 'in the natural'. The eyes of their hearts are closed.

Two interesting connective stories to the text cited are the stories of the healing of blind Bartimaeus and the healing of the lame man in the book of John. The disciples saw Bartimaeus' blindness as a curse. In response to their question, (see St. John Chapter 9), Jesus responded by saying: "Neither hath this man sinned, nor his parents: but that *the works of God should be made manifest in him.*" With the case of the man lame from birth, after he was healed, Jesus found him and told him: "Go and sin no more less a worse thing happens to you."

Some situations may be for a manifestation of the works of God. Jesus said that Lazarus sickness was for "the works of God to be made manifest." There was a plan. God never works haphazardly. Part of the plan was for Jesus to wait four days. By so doing, the stage was being set for the manifestation of the works of God.

But, let's go back to the stories of the blind and lame man. The blind man had done nothing to cause his blindness. However, the lame man was cautioned to go and sin no more. In matters of health and healing, we tend to judge from what we can see and even conjecture about what we do not know.

Some situations may be unto death and others may be for a manifestation of the works of God. In any case, those who are healed do eventually die. Only God Himself knows what He is working behind the scenes! He says: I know the plans I have for you!! (See Jeremiah 29:11) God knows!! We simply have to trust His Word. He told Martha: 'If you only *believe* you would see *the works of God.*'

We cannot put God in a box when it comes to how He will work. We may want God to 'quick fix' us when simple lifestyle changes could be the answer for longevity. Namaan almost missed his blessing because he did not think he needed to do anything to participate in his healing process. We can either limit God by our preconceived ideas because we demand a 'fireworks' 'call it done' display of His power or we can also limit Him by our 'Lilliputian faith![38]

****

---

[38] The Lilliputians were the very short inhabitants of Lilliput in the novel Gulliver's Travels. So our faith can be diminutive akin to the height, or lack thereof, of the Lilliputians

Disaster or Design

———•◦❀◦•———

Your eyes saw my unformed substance, and in Your book all the days [of my life] were written before ever they took shape, when as yet there was none of them. How precious and weighty also are your thoughts to me, O God! How vast is the sum of them! Psalm 139:16 & 17 Amplified Version

Gideon must have wondered how God would have him win a battle with only three hundred men. Would it not turn out disastrously? The Israelites, as they approached the Red Sea, with an enraged enemy hot on their trail, may have pondered whether this would not have been the end for them.

God never works in a 'willy nilly' fashion and faith simply has to take God at His word. Thankfully, God has the recipe for my life and as we know recipes call for a number of different things, combined in the correct proportions. If I tried to write a recipe for my own life, I am sure I would make a mess of things. Thankfully, God is in charge. In His superior wisdom, He will not have to experiment or operate on a basis of trial and error.

I smile when I recollect my debut with my recipe for making cou-cou. Yes, it was trial and error, emphasis on error. Here is an excerpt from Prayer Letter # 52, written in July 2009:

How can I forget when I failed to follow a recipe I had been given to make cou-cou? Flying fish and cou-cou is considered to be our national dish. Most Barbadian women therefore pride themselves on being able to 'turn a good cou-cou.' I was not to be left out. I wanted to 'try my hand' and surprise my husband, who had never known me to make cou-cou. His mother was an excellent cou-cou maker so we frequently benefited from her culinary skills.

On that memorable day, I joyfully turned my cou-cou and it looked good. I wanted it to be very creamy, you know, mellow and smooth, just like my mother-in-law's. I followed the instructions given, well..... for the most part. But I decided to add more and more of the okra water to increase the cou-cou's mellowness. I had the flasks ready into which I would place the cou-cou. Andy would have it nice and hot when he arrived at home. Mummy Estwick's cou-cou always came out in a nice symmetrical ball which gently tumbled out of the flask. While putting the cou-cou into the flask, I momentarily pondered its slightly soft consistency. However, I felt that in the flask it would more or less congeal.

The moment arrived. I did not tell Andy what a wonderful meal awaited him. I wanted to see his eyes twinkle with surprise and pleasure. I remember that evening very vividly. For some reason there was a little gathering around the table. The children looked on, eagerly like me, to see Daddy's face. Removing the cover, Andy took up the flask and tilted it.

Much to my consternation, yeah horror, instead of a well-rounded symmetrical ball of cou-cou, what gushed forth was a thick, lava type substance which galloped madly to the plate's edge. Maybe, it was its viscous nature which prevented the contents from cascading on to the table's surface. There was a momentary silence as we gaped at the flattened mushy spectacle which bore very remote resemblance to what Mummy Estwick produced!

Suppressed tittering eventually gave way to unrestrained outbursts of belly aching laughter. Andy surveyed the cooled lava and decided that it was not edible. Not even for the cat. We turned my mangled sloshy efforts into the bin. Enough for surprises and ironic twists! There was an encore however which did not end disastrously, as I followed the recipe more carefully. When we stick to God's recipe for our lives, I think we can get some wonderful surprises. I expect that when God turns me out, I will not be a disaster!

END OF EXTRACT

I absolutely revel in Romans 8:28 which tells us that all things work together for good to those who love God. Standing next to Romans 8:28 is Jeremiah 29:11. Here God declares that He knows the plans that He has for us... and they are good plans. I have always commented that God knows, not my friends or church family, not even my biological family, God alone knows His plans for me. He wrote them in my Book of Life even before I was born. What a stirring thought!

Sometimes, God will share part of His secret plan with us. See Proverbs 25:14 and Proverbs 3:32. When we love God, He can give us a little scoop on what He is up to – His design for us. You never share a secret with someone with whom you are not intimate. Sometimes when God shares secret plans and dreams with us, it might be best to keep them to ourselves because they may seem incomprehensible and foolish to an unbeliever.

Joseph shared his dreams with his brothers and we know the result. However, Joseph intuitively knew that God had a plan and strategy for bringing to fruition his dreams. He acknowledges the excellence of God's design when he could eventually tell his brothers in Genesis 50:20:

But as for you, ye thought evil against me, but God meant it unto good, to bring to pass, as it is this day, to save much people alive.

Being sold into slavery and then being imprisoned wrongfully appeared disastrous. However, those apparent negatives were in fact pivotal to God's long term strategizing. When with carnal vision, when we look at a person's life and circumstances, we may see the underside of the tapestry of his /her life which would look quite mysterious and maybe confusing, but on the upper side there is an intricate design which only God can see as He works the loom.

Carlyle B. Haynes in his book On The Throne of the World says that nothing goes wrong in the life of a Christian. It would be great if you could read the chapter where he develops that point with exquisite spiritual insight. It may require a paradigm shift in your thinking.

Joseph's life epitomes the irrevocable truth of Romans 8:28 and our lives, as Christians, who love and trust God, can do the same. Many centuries have passed but God has not changed and He can indeed make all things work together for good and perfect that thing which concerns us. See Psalm 138:8. He is the best Design Artist ever! Wow!

****

Supersizing Your Faith

---◦❈◦---

*You don't have enough faith," Jesus told them.
"I tell you the truth, if you had faith even as
small as a mustard seed, you could say to
this mountain, 'Move from here to there,' and
it would move. Nothing would be impossible.*
Matthew 17:20 NLT

We all start out with a *measure of faith*. '...according as God hath
dealt to every man the measure of faith'. (See Romans 12:3) The
choice is ours – to tuck it away in a napkin, and be content to
admire the faith we see in others, or to invest what we have. But
how in the world can you invest your faith? Investments, as you
know involve some measure of risk.

It is God who provides us opportunities to invest our faith by
what He sends or allows through His providential workings. You
may be surprised to know that one of the methods is through
adversity. We may well wonder if He could not find some more
'palatable' way to increase or strengthen our faith – one that does
not involve any kind of discomfort. The Apostle James gives a
paradoxical command.

> *My brethren, count it all joy when ye fall into divers
> temptations; Knowing* this, *that the trying of your
> faith worketh patience. But let patience have* her

perfect work, that ye may be perfect and entire, wanting nothing. James1:2-4 KJV

Dr. Barry Black in his book *The Blessing of Adversity* uses the expression 'supersizing your faith'. He advocates, and I agree with this foundational statement:

To supersize your faith, accept God's plan for your life. His purposes for us are better than anything we can plan for ourselves, for He is omniscient – all-wise and all-knowing. He knows how long we will live and what will bring us the greatest joy. His amazing love for us can bring us to our desired destination (Jeremiah 29:11); but because we have free will, God's ideal purpose is linked to our faithfulness. He will not force us on the narrow road that leads to life (Matthew 7: 13-14), though He seeks to do for us more than we can imagine (Ephesians 3:20).[39]

What Dr. Black says is absolutely true! I am very excited about God's plan for my life. Out of His awesome strategic plan He has enabled me to creatively recount my health and spiritual adventure with Him, which when properly packaged, can be a help and blessing to others who want to grow in their faith experience with Him.

In 2003, I made a defining decision which changed the trajectory of my life. Thankfully, I have always known that my life is in God's hands and under His eagle eye supervision. (See Psalm 31:15) It gives one a great internal peace and comfort to know that nothing touches the child of God, except it first passes

---

[39] Barry Black, *The Blessing of Adversity*, Tyndale House Publishers Inc., Literary Agency of Life Media, New York, NY (2011) p 119

through the hands of God. To really supersize your faith, it is imperative that you believe this. Because our human nature is wired for 'flowery beds of ease', we balk at the thought that:

> *Acceptance of God's plan may force us to drink a bitter cup. It might lead us to the way of the Cross, taking us through Gethsemane to Calvary to a tomb ...we should feel certain that God makes no mistakes. His plans are flawless, His purposes sure. Knowing this can empower us to pray the perfect prayer: "Your will be done".* [40]

Flowery beds of ease and epicurean living (eat and drink, for tomorrow we die) are antithetical to the 'way of the cross'. It will grate against our nature. But, if we are really to supersize our faith we need an entire revamping of our thinking, our way of seeing the world, and the interpretation of the events of our lives. In fact, we need a new heart altogether! It is the Word of God, and specifically, *the promises found in the Word* which will help us to move from a raisin shrivelled faith to one that allows us to 'step out of the boat'. One spiritual writer says:

> *In them (the promises of God's Word) He is speaking to us individually, speaking as directly as if we could listen to His voice. It is in these promises that Christ communicates to us His grace and power. They are leaves from that tree which is "for the healing of the nations." Received, assimilated, they are to be the strength of the character, the inspiration and sustenance of the life.* [41]

---

[40] Ellen G. White, *The Faith I Live By* (Review and Herald Publishing Association, Washington, D.C (1958) P 220

[41] Ibid p 9

I have never heard God's voice literally but I have heard it in my heart, in the depths of my soul, as He has repeated to me certain specific and personal promises like Jeremiah 32:40 and 41, verses which constituted my initial Rhema. The promises, *received and assimilated*, allow us to move out of our comfort zone. But to be honest, a comfort zone speaks for itself, it is comfortable! We love our warm fuzzy blankets and do not want to be exposed to any kind of 'cold'. But, as reality would have it, you *cannot* remain in your comfort zone and still supersize your faith. *You simply cannot have your cake and eat it too.*

There is certainly divine wisdom in the 'way of the cross'. Everyone is included in the plan of salvation. It is God's intent that *all* be saved but we cannot presumptuously determine the method of salvation. Though we may want to have our cake, Heaven, and still eat it, enjoy the flowery beds of ease all our lives, the two are not compatible. And, there is a reason: This insightful writer notes:

> *How easy would be the way to heaven if there was no self-denial or cross! How worldlings would rush in the way, and hypocrites would travel in it without number! Thank God for the cross, the self-denial.*[42]

So getting out of the boat will cost us something... our warm fuzzy blankets of security and a life of predictable sameness. And yes, there a risk is involved, humanly speaking, but never with God! He is not a casino God! When you step out of the boat, one of two things will occur, *depending on whether you are stepping out under the guidance and directorship of God, or you are doing so impulsively, on your own steam*: You will either drown in doubt or you will walk in faith gear...on the water.

---

[42] Ellen G. White, *Our Father Cares*, Review and Herald Publishing Association, Washington, DC 20039 (1992) P 288

So we can take our whitened knuckles off the side of the boat and let go...and let God...

We don't need to panic because the *bona fide* faith traveller knows how to walk supernaturally to a God who is above His laws and can defy the laws of physics to honour the faith of His son or daughter who will dare, based on the inscrutable promises of the Word, to have a supersized faith which does not stagger! (See Romans 4:19 and Job 13:15)

****

Demanding The Spectacular

But Naaman went away angry and said, "I thought that he would surely come out to me and stand and call on the name of the LORD his God, wave his hand over the spot and cure me of my leprosy. Are not Abana and Pharpar, the rivers of Damascus, better than all the waters of Israel? Couldn't I wash in them and be cleansed?" So he turned and went off in a rage. 2 Kings 5:11 & 12 NIV

Leprosy! That dreaded disease afflicted Naaman. He was told about the healing powers of the prophet Elisha and he decided to go to him, fully expecting a dramatic and spectacular healing. However, his preconceived ideas of what Elisha would do were dashed to the ground. The anti-climax was more than he could bear. His expectations, however, revealed the pride that was hidden in his heart. Possibly, he found the instructions given to be of an insulting nature to a man of his stature. How dare Elijah not treat him with more deference! He was ready to stomp away in a fit. Read the full details in 2 Kings 5:1-13.

Fortunately, Naaman was challenged to reconsider his decision and common sense reigned. His attendants advised him that since it was such a simple thing he had been asked to do, he should at least try it. Dismounting his high horse of pride and arrogance, he decided to obey the prophet's explicit instructions.

Naaman had to dip, not once, nor twice, but *seven* times in the Jordan River. Six times would not even suffice. It was when he made the seventh dip that he came up restored, just as the prophet Elisha had predicted.

So, what relevant lessons does this story have for us? There may be many, but I will highlight two which are critical in the context of recounting my journey. Most of us expect miracles of healing to be of a spectacular nature. Some folk can envisage no other kind. Possibly, some people may die while looking for the spectacular while healing was in their reach.

Like Naaman, I was expecting something spectacular – a miracle from the blue! I wanted instantaneous correction of whatever was going awry with my body, as indicated by the growth of the fibroids and the unexplained weight loss. The morning after my visit to the naturopathic practitioner, during my 'quiet time', I read time this divinely orchestrated information:

> *God's miracles do not always bear the outward resemblance of miracles. Often they are brought about in a way which looks like the natural course of events... We answer our own prayers by using the remedies within our reach... Natural means used in accordance with God's will bring about supernatural results...We cannot expect the Lord to work a miracle for us while we neglect the simple remedies He has provided for our use, which aptly and opportunely applied, will bring about a miraculous result.*[43]

That comment helped to reposition my thinking on what a miracle could be. I definitely did not want to miss the forest for the trees.

---

[43] Ellen G. White, *Selected Messages Book 2*, Review and Herald Publishing Association, Hagerstown, MD (1958) p 346

How easy it is to do that!! Admittedly, I somehow imbibed the notion that the approach was to 'pray and call it done', and that was all to it. I could then lap my feet. Such naivety!

The other very important thing which God showed me was that our interest is mainly in physical healing, but God is after more than the physical, He is after our soul's salvation and our complete spiritual healing. He wants to heal all of us, our tongues, our attitudes and our crooked thinking about some matters.

****

Straight Talk

———•❊•———

He said, "If you will listen carefully to the voice of the LORD your God and do what is right in his sight, obeying his commands and keeping all his decrees, then I will not make you suffer any of the diseases I sent on the Egyptians; for I am the LORD who heals you."
Exodus 15:26 NLT

Namaan had to do a simple thing, which he initially balked at doing. He wanted the prophet to just speak a word and 'fix him' one time. But that was not to be, he had to play his part. We also have our part to play in our healing.

The application of the principles of faith in the realm of health and healing may be so misinterpreted and contorted that much confusion, deception and disappointment result. We are disappointed because our dear Mary was prayed for and it was called 'done', but all that occurred after that 'prayer of faith' which demanded her healing is that (to use Bajan vernacular) 'she gone and dun dead'.

The Bible warns us about our hearts. They are described as being deceitful and desperately wicked. (See Jeremiah 17:9.) The first person the heart will deceive *is its owner*. We all need a heart transplant so that we can better understand the issues before us.

When it comes to healing and faith, some people's idea is that all you need to do is to 'believe', whatever that may mean to them. In some cases, simple belief is all that is necessary, as shown in many Biblical examples where Jesus and His disciples healed people. However, there are variables and factors which make each person's case different. It is imperative that we bear in mind that God will *always* act in the best interest of the person, respecting the choices which he makes in order to handle his health situation. In our human arrogance, we cannot dictate to God how He must act. After all, *He* is God!

Though God can and does act in astounding miraculous fashion, it is never to replace our efforts, where such will assist us in answering our own prayers. I am thrilled that my country Barbados promotes a healthy lifestyle via its educational programmes on the media. The information disseminated is designed to sensitize us to the part we must play in preserving our most precious treasure — our health.

We are constantly admonished to change our lifestyle by making adjustments in our eating habits. We have been advised to cut down on fatty, greasy foods, decrease our sugar and salt intake, and drink more water. We are also encouraged to engage in some form of exercise. Much of the advice may fall on deaf ears until we become like Paul.

'Paul' is our fictional character as we hypothesize for a moment. Let's consider his case. Paul is enjoying 'good' health. He eats and drinks as he pleases, ignoring all the warnings given to him on the media. Or, he may not be eating 'so bad' after all. He just indulges in junk food occasionally, which could be twice a week. He argues: '*All things* in moderation'. He may even scoff and sneer at those who are trying to eat a little better with a sarcastic: "Yah gaw dead someday".

Suddenly Paul starts to experience disturbing changes in his body. They are sudden to him, but they were in fact gradually occurring for quite a while, but their *manifestation* was sudden. So while he was sneering and mocking those who were making their little efforts to change, he had no idea what was occurring in the dark cavern of *his* body.

He becomes alarmed. His first thought is that whatever is wrong, he wants it fixed immediately. He considers two options. He could either go to the doctor, securing a miracle drug that will correct the situation as quickly as possible or, better yet, he could go to his religious leader and request a prayer for healing. That would definitely be a more prompt solution. He would not have to change anything or do anything except 'believe'.

As it relates to Paul's scenario and his quick fix attitude, here are some rhetorical questions I would ask: Should Paul not be advised to pay attention to the health laws he would have broken, which may have contributed to the changes in his body? By the way, heredity is not destiny! Should Paul be made to feel that he can claim the healing promises in the Word of God while living in direct transgression of the laws of nature and the laws of his being? Would this not in essence be encouraging in him an attitude of presumption?

Faith's counterfeit is presumption. Sometimes they may seem to wear the same garb, but one is a wily imposter. How can we distinguish between them? This timely quotation gives at least one principle of differentiation:

> *Those who bring their petitions to God, claiming His promise while they do not comply with the conditions, insult Jehovah. They bring the name of Christ as their authority for the fulfillment of the*

*promise, but they do not those things that would
show faith in Christ and love for Him.*[44]

This is straight talk now! Paul is representative of many of us.
Sometimes to save our very lives, God has to sit us down and
give us some straight talk. He does not prevaricate. He wants us
to understand some critical things which may require a paradigm
shift in our thinking. I have been given sound, sensible and
reasonable counsel which I have taken to heart. For example, I
have been sensitized to the fact that "the laws of nature, as truly
as the precepts of the Decalogue, are divine and that only in
obedience to them can health be recovered or preserved."[45]

Here is more straight talk:

> *Those who seek healing by prayer should not neglect
> to make use of the remedial agencies within their
> reach. It is not a denial of faith to use such remedies
> as God has provided to alleviate pain and to aid
> nature in her work of restoration.*[46]

The unadulterated truth is that going a natural route in response
to a health issue will require time, effort, discipline, courage and
stamina, and of course faith. It could never be an overnight thing.
How in the world could we expect that changes which have taken
years to occur can be corrected in a few days? Making changes
require self-denial, self-sacrifice and a dogged, undaunted
approach to the task at hand. Some of the critics will not even
have the guts for this. Changing your lifestyle will be a challenge

---

[44] Ellen G. White, *Christ's Object Lessons*, Review and Herald Publishing
Association, Washington, D.C. (1900) p 143

[45] Ellen G. White, *The Ministry of Healing*, Pacific Press Publishing Association,
1350 Villa Street, Mountain View, California 94042, (1905) p 113

[46] Ibid, p. 231

because you have to do battle with appetite and long held suicidal practices. The quick fix is much easier.

God also gives us straight talk about His power and His willingness to help us. Isaiah 41:10 assures us that God will not leave us in the lurch. All His biddings are His enablings.

****

Protected in God's Pavilion

Thou shalt hide them in the secret of thy presence from the pride of man:

thou shalt keep them secretly in a pavilion from the strife of tongues. Psalms 31:20

Thou preparest a table before me in the presence of mine enemies, thou anointest my head with oil; my cup runneth over. Psalm 23:5

But no weapon that is formed against you shall prosper, and every tongue that shall rise against you in judgment you shall show to be in the wrong. This [peace, righteousness, security, triumph over opposition] is the heritage of the servants of the Lord [those in whom the ideal Servant of the Lord is reproduced]; this is the righteousness or the vindication which they obtain from Me [this is that which I impart to them as their justification], says the Lord. Isaiah 54:17 Amplified Bible

The versatility of the Word of God is amazing. It simply leaves you open mouthed as you experience its flexibility as it curves to fit every aspect of your experience. Human nature has not

150

changed, so the same protection God provided for David against His enemies is still in place today.

As I shared at that memorable Hymnspeak service in 2008, the path of faith will invite curious onlookers. The enemies of faith, as manifested in the clairvoyant spectators, the soothsayers, naysayers and doomsday predictors will have their say. Lysa Terkeurst in her book: *What Happens When Women Say Yes to God* comments:

> *Becoming a woman who unashamedly says yes to God will cause you to be different from many of your family members and friends....While not all your friends and family will be naysayers, some will. The difference naysayers see in you compels them to come against you full force because Christ working through you will sometimes step on the toes of their consciences. While naysayers may talk a good Christian game, they deny Christ in their attitude and actions towards others. Instead of allowing those feelings of conviction to produce good changes in them, they seek to discourage you in the hopes of hushing Christ in you.*[47]

From the outset, God told me to let my expectation be from Him. (See Psalm 62:6) As a result of taking that advice to heart, I have been protected against cynicism at what I have termed "the incongruities of Christian behaviour."

I have always been a quiet and reserved person, certainly not an exhibitionist. Obeying the divine fiat to share my experience verbally and also in writing pushed me from my comfort zone. It

[47] Lysa Terkeurst, *What Happens When Women Say Yes to God*, Harvest House Publishers, Eugene, Oregon 97402 (2007) p 78

certainly placed me in a position of vulnerability, but I was not thrown to the wolves.

Gossip abounds everywhere and no place is excluded!! We can learn to handle it with grace and keep growing. *Genuine faith will be attacked!* Its attackers know not what they do. But why should the traveller on a walk of genuine faith and trust in God be ridiculed? There are several reasons, but key among them would be the fact that the traveller's wisdom and common sense are being called into question.

God will not uphold folly and presumption. But for the genuine faith traveller, He will prepare a table right in the presence of enemies and the setting is in the valley of the shadow of death. (See Psalm 23) From the metaphor, we can correctly infer that God will meet all of our needs, prospering us right before those who have taken up the position of 'enemies'.

God places His children in a pavilion from the strife of tongues, so that no weapon formed against us can prosper. If as Christians we *believed and lived* these words, if we should ever come into a situation where we are centre stage for gossip, we would never be dismayed or depressed by unfavourable comments.

Like Nehemiah, the faith traveller must keep focused and not come down to parley with critics.(See Nehemiah Chapter 6: 3 & 4) We should not be distracted by the talk, but simply keep walking, by God's grace, humbly with our God. (See Micah 6:8). Faith and presumption may seem to wear similar garb but as Shakespeare says:

> *Angels are bright still, though the brightest fell.*
> *Though all things foul would wear the brows of*
> *grace, Yet grace must still look so.*[48]

---

[48] Macbeth Act 4 Scene 3

In other words, all behaviour that would *appear* to be genuine faith may not be that; it may simply be presumption cleverly disguised. Despite presumption's slanderous mimicking of faith, she can do no other but to come naked and take her blows. When the enemies of faith have ceased their battering, she remains standing firm, stronger than ever. (See 1 John 5:4)

Isaiah 41:11 tells us the end result of our enemies. God has a plan for dealing with them all, so we can relax and keep fighting the *correct* fight! The Bible says that those who come against us will come *one* way but flee in *seven* different ways! (See Deuteronomy 28:7)

****

No Façade... 'De Real Ting'!

---·❖·---

The joy of the Lord is my strength. Nehemiah 8:10

It is said: To lose joy is to lose everything. A true word indeed: A merry heart doeth good like a medicine; but a broken spirit drieth the bones. Proverbs 17:22

It is no wonder that God says that He would make our bones fat! The joy of the Lord is a joy the Lord gives, not man. What is fascinating about it is that it becomes even more radiant in the storm. Quite a paradox! The joy most folk experience emanate from their circumstances. And indeed, we do have joyous occasions in our lives: times we laugh and have great fun and are proud of our own accomplishments or those of our family and friends.

But now, what about when a situation, in and of itself, does not generate its own joy? But yet we are joyful and skipping merrily along to the amazement of clairvoyant spectators. That kind of joy comes from one source. Is it possible to have it? I think so and this translates into strength. Not ours, but God's strength in us. How else can we explain Paul and Silas singing and praising God, of all places, in prison?

So clearly joy is not some 'skin yah teet' façade but a real deep and abiding assurance in the goodness of God. Such a joy allows you to be a real person. You can shed a tear and still be joyful. Nothing equals the joy of knowing that you are in the centre of God's will for your life, nothing equals the joy of knowing that all things are working together for your good. Nothing equals the joy of seeing God perform some awesome moves – moves that would stun the skeptics and agnostics.

On May 8, 2006, I stood in the aisle of a Delta Flight, thousands of miles above the ocean … and hugged a young lady. It was a spectacular Jabez Appointment. We were shocked beyond belief! Heather Moore, a former Christ Church Foundation School student, had not seen me in twenty years! It was in 1984, her last year at school when we parted and had absolutely no contact whatsoever until that day we met.

She had dreamt about me and wanted to make contact with me. Her dream was fulfilled as we sat and engaged in a dialogue which had been supernaturally planned for us. That entire, absolutely incredible, divinely orchestrated meeting is documented in Prayer Letter #28 entitled: *An Amazing Appointment.* Talk about adventure!!

Attached to the joy that comes from God is a sense of humour. Many of the folk in congregations with whom I shared my experiences will recollect that they laughed heartily when I recounted certain aspects of my journey, especially the 'Intruder Incident.' That incident is very vividly described in Prayer Letter #5. There I explain the concept of prolepsis. Even in that potentially dangerous incident there was humour in my recounting of it.

All in all, if you know God, then you will know that He has a sense of humour Himself and loves to make us laugh. In His presence is fullness of joy! Who would not want to walk in the joy of the Lord? How do we acquire the power to do it? Just walk in faith and… believe the Word!

****

Still Waters... Run Deep!

---•◉•---

In quietness and confidence is your strength.
Isaiah 30:15 NIV

This text is one of my favourites because it seems to characterize me. I have always been a rather quiet person. My confidence is not in myself but in what God can do for me. I met God in the 21st year of my life and my confidence in Him has steadily grown. Among those most best acquainted with you, would be your students. Over the past thirty four years I have interacted with thousands of students who can attest to the fact that I do tend to be a rather calm and quiet type of person. I do not think it is merely a personality trait, I see it as a blessing from God.

The storms of life cannot ruffle a calm spirit which knows how to rest in God. Quiet people are often misunderstood. But as I often like to say, quietness is not synonymous with stupidity or weakness. Many years ago, at a staff meeting, my former Principal, the late Major Hugh Barker, said: "Nola is a gentle giant".

My confidence in God has grown over the years. I know Him to be a Man of His word. (See Numbers 23:19 and Psalm 89:34) I believe that we honour God when we show that we have confidence in Him and His plan for our lives.

****

The Litmus Test: According to His Will

And this is the confidence that we have in him; that, if we ask any thing according to his will, he heareth us: And if we know that he hear us, whatsoever we ask, we know that we have the petitions that we desired of him.
1 John 5:14 & 15

These verses represent some of the strongest pillars on which our houses of faith are built. There is nothing obscure about the words; there is no imagery that we need to decipher. It simply speaks of the confidence we can have in God, indicating that if we believe that God has heard our request, then we can be assured that we have what we have requested.

However, since our human nature is deceitful and tricky, there certainly are some cautions. Those verses refer I believe, to those who are disciples. Furthermore, the text is not a 'carte blanc' for us to ask any and everything. If God granted all of our unsanctified requests, it would not be in our best interest. So, embedded in the text is that very important caveat, 'according to His will'. Four words which make all the difference between faith and presumption.

Though not explicitly stated, the issue of timing is to be inferred from this text. God tells us that we have (present tense) the petition. Yet, God has the right to decide when we may actually see the thing, whatever it is, with our physical eyes. How can you be in possession of something you do not see? We glibly mouth, "Faith is the substance of things hoped for, the evidence of things *not seen.*"

It is at this critical point, that the tunnel of faith narrows, exclusively so. Those who must always see evidence of an answered prayer before they believe, will find the tunnel is too narrow for them to traverse. They will turn back, as well as those who must always see a light. Enveloped in the blackness of their own doubt, they will retreat.

The tunnel of faith narrows for those who have never grasped the spiritual truth of the importance of agreeing with what *God* has said. John Eldredge in his book *Walking With God* says some very deep things, certainly worth thinking about.

> *We don't believe the Scriptures because they don't seem to align with what we are feeling right now... we are so stubborn in our unbelief because we aren't at that moment experiencing, whatever it is God says is true... We cannot base our convictions on whether or not we are seeing or experiencing the truth of what God says. It is an arrogant posture, to let our state of being be the judge of whether the Scripture is true for us.*[49]

It is quite possible that many folk base their faith on their feelings. However, feelings can be quite variable and cannot sustain you on a long journey. Only those who have learnt to stand on God's Word *alone*, not their feelings, will continue, finding that their faith has so expanded that the tunnel is no longer narrow.

---

[49] John Eldredge, <u>Walking With God.</u> Nashville Tenesssee, Thomas Nelson Inc. p 100,101

Many must see to believe. In that 2008 Hymnspeak presentation, I noted that our prayers can be answered in the supernatural realm *before* they are manifested in the physical realm. The carnal mind cannot fathom that. If God has said something will happen, then there is no question as to the fulfilment of His word. Our part is to believe!

****

Chronos or Kairos

Wait on the Lord: be of good courage, and he shall strengthen thine heart: wait, I say, on the Lord. Psalm 27:14

Yea, let none that wait on thee be ashamed: let them be ashamed which transgress without cause. Psalm 25:3

Many of us are just plain impatient. We want it and we want it now. Thankfully, we cannot bulldoze God into operating in our chronos time frame. That impatient spirit can actually thwart God's perfect plan for our lives. In matters of health and healing, most remarkably, is this spirit of 'I want it done now' manifested. We like quick fixes because we do not want to go through anything. We want the prayer to call 'it done' and it be done instantaneously. Who cares about learning lessons or reasoning from cause to effect?

But at times, God waits. God responds in His 'kairos' time. God has a specific time frame in which He will move. He waits so that He can be more gracious to us and while we are waiting He strengthens our heart. Once God gives a word, (See Isa 30:21) you can wait comfortably, going about your business in calm assurance that 'it is done while it is being done.'

In 2003, as I prayed about my decision regarding my health, God led me to read in my Streams in The Desert devotional prayer journal a most candid response. The concept of 'it is done while it is being done' emerged. The unfolding years enabled me to understand the deep lesson God was teaching me. I was about quick fixes at first, not about any lessons.

Soon after my anointing at my home in August 2003, (I was impressed to engage in that Biblically sound action) I told my First Elder at the time, Gregory Hallet, to reserve a Sunday for me to have my praise session at church. I just knew God would swoop down and drop an instantaneous miracle in my lap. God must have quietly chuckled at my naivety and fallacious thinking.

The 'done while being done' concept speaks to the issue of process and product. Our carnal nature wants the end product immediately; we tend to despise the process. But the infallible wisdom of God knows that we need the process even more than we need the product. To bless us instantly with the product would, for some, invite nothing less than an attitude of presumption.

There is much we do not immediately perceive in that impatient attitude, that resistance to waiting on God. Hidden is an attitude of not accepting culpability. Why me? Our bodies are very resilient and can take abuse for a long time. But should anything go awry, we want a degenerative process which may have taken several years to occur, to be repaired in a week or a month. Who wants to reason from cause to effect? No, whatever went wrong has nothing whatsoever to do with us! So why should we wait? There is nothing to learn. God in love and tender mercy will not foster an attitude of presumption in us; however, the enemy with crafty subtlety will.

Quite frankly, can any of us say that we have never broken the laws of health? A better question might be: Are we aware that such laws even exist? We have all broken the laws of health and the laws of our being, either deliberately or ignorantly. None of us can justifiably claim innocence.

So, why does God wait and not drop a miracle bomb on us? The waiting helps us to see our blind spots and to make amends. The Word says that those who wait on God are blessed and will not be made ashamed. I have facetiously said that no one has had to offer me any "smelling salts". While we are waiting the enemies of faith, who may felt that we stepped out on a presumptuous branch, and therefore silently retreated, are also waiting. I chuckled very heartily at the versatility of God's word as I read Psalm 41:8-12.

There is one tremendous benefit of waiting on God, which in itself, turns out to be a kind of vindication. The Word says that those who wait on God will have their strength renewed and they will mount up wings as eagles. Their hearts will also be strengthened. These are promises from God. We cannot renew our own strength, so if we are truly waiting on God, then we should be waiting in strength and not stress!

Abraham is an example of what it means to wait. He waited for the promised child for many years – until it was an impossible situation. We can barely wait a year or two, far less several years. But when God waits, it is always for some specific purpose. Isaiah 30:18 suggests one of His purposes. God has every right to have His full share of glory. *It would be a crying shame to rob Him!!*

(The book: *When God Waits: Making Sense of Divine Delays* by Jerome Daley would be a very helpful book to read. You may Google it.) Thank you for your gift Brother Gordon!

****

The 'Waiting Game'

---·◈·---

Therefore the Lord waits to be gracious to you, and therefore he exalts himself to show mercy to you. For the Lord is a God of justice; blessed are all those who wait for him. Isaiah 30:18 ESV

God in His infinite wisdom does not always answer our prayers in the manner and time we expect. He delays His answer, as it were, to test our faith and for various other reasons. I know that God is not playing games with us when He waits, so there is intentional irony in the title. We are the ones who need to 'play our game right' and wait peacefully on God.

Metaphorically speaking, God can choose to put us in His waiting room. What should we do while we are there? Should we pace up and down, frantically biting our nails, waiting for the sword of Damocles to descend upon us? Not in the least bit! We can creatively engage ourselves and learn our deepest life lessons.

Over ten years ago, when I knew God would invite me into His waiting room, I gave a presentation at my church which I captioned: *In God's Waiting Room.* For me, it was a deep message. However, to the casual listener it may have seemed like just another one of *those sermons.* I can still reflect on the notes I made.

Mary and Martha went into God's waiting room for four days before Jesus came to their aid. It was not a callous wait but one of studied deliberation. There was purpose behind it. If for some reason God puts us in a waiting room concerning some aspect of our lives we have committed to Him, then we must occupy ourselves in the waiting time. God is *never inactive*. He is always working behind the scenes on those things which we have committed to Him. That is, if we have *truly committed* them to God and did not immediately snatch them back out of His hands, after an obligatory and cosmetic prayer.

While we are in God's waiting room, and in a teachable mode, we can feast our eyes on the walls around us which are decorated with choice words, like apples of gold in pictures of silver. (See Proverbs 25:11.) The promises of God are emblazoned in those picture frames. We have enough of them, over 3000 to engage our attention.

While we are waiting, there is a silent group also waiting. I have called them *'The Watchers'* which is the title of one of my 'valley' poems. The 'watchers' would be those who may not understand the ways of God, or the life of faith and what it entails. This 'waiting' of the watchers is of a different nature.

At some point in our Christian experience we may all come into an experience where we are centre stage for onlookers. It may be family troubles, a change in health, a broken marriage, some distressing situation with our children, or even financial disaster. We never know when we may have a reversal of life's status quo. Not even the watchers know when it may be their turn.

It is part of human nature to be spectators and commentators. Psalm 41:7 & 8 speak about those who whisper and surmise. While we wait, God miraculously hides us in His pavilion from the strife of tongues.

Reality and deep truth can be couched in a garb of satirical humour. As is acknowledged, 'Many a serious thing is said in a jest.' God has indeed blessed me with a creative sense of wit. A merry heart does do its job!! I have extracted from my archives a favourite poem *Duh Waiting*:

Valley Collection Poem--- 'Duh Waiting'
Composed: November 27, 2005

Yes, duh waiting fuh me to collapse
Not a malicious desire but a vague expectation
Cause I step out de box and could be wrong
Blaps! Drop down to de ground
Me and my faith reduced to a poor pitiful mound.
Wuh she playing doh?
Talking bout God lead she pun some other path
Wuh law! I got to laugh
Cause some people does 'car' dis religion ting too far
Duh wishing pun a star
Cuh dear, God gi we common sense
At nuh expense
So we en got to ask He to direct we here and dere
We got sense enough we own self to steer.

Hmmm! well lemme tell dum sum ting
I as blind as a bat.
So I got to ask God: 'Which way to turn? Dis or dat?
Plus, he dun tell me if ya lack wisdom, 'Ask me
I does give it way fuh free'
Some people real wise and know wuh to do
But I tell yah, duh en got a clue!
Duh tie up in a box
Dem en know that God smarter and more
clever than the proverbial fox!!

Leh dum wait and "wizzy wizzy"
But my God and I busy busy!!!
Doing dixie in de valley
"Come," He says, 'Leh we dally!
I hay standing still
Cause God routing de enemy
Every promise He gun fulfill
He dun say in de Word dat
Dem who dare to wait pun He
He gun make all duh enemies flee
He say deh en gun be confounded
In fact the skeptics and agnostics
will be left astounded
So leh dum wait
Tinking duh know my fate
Yeah.... right!
Nola.....de late!
Leh dum wait fuh me to collapse
Brax!
De rocking chair of peace God put me in
Is a cool place to relax!
When ya dare to obey God's Rhema Word to ya heart
Expect de talk to start
But sistah don doubt! God does finish wuh ever He start.
Once God in de canoe wid you
De rapids you will ford with dexterity and finesse
Cause God don mess
He will rain down and bless
All a we who prepared to stan de test!!!

****

Awesome Prolepsis!

---•❖•---

For the angel of the LORD is a guard; he
surrounds and defends all who fear him.
Psalm 34:7 NLT

Do you believe in the ministry of angels? I certainly do!! You are more probably more familiar with the King James Version of this text because most of us know it by heart and it is the favourite of many Christians. I call this 'midnight adventure' *The Intruder Incident.* That is the night, or more accurately, very early the morning of December 1, 2003, that I believe with all my heart that my guardian angel stood next to me.

This incident is one of the most uncanny of my journey. Not to leave you in absolute suspense, let me give you some brief details. More important though that the actual details of the encounter is the message behind the incident, as well as its juxtaposition with another significant event. Providential orchestration is another way God directs our steps.

On awaking at minutes to two o' clock to use the bathroom, I discovered someone crouched on my stairs. Thinking it was my daughter who may have fallen ill and was coming to fetch me, I turned on the light only to discover it was a man!!!

Shock! Amazement! But no screams from me. Just silence. He was silent too. But he knew he was discovered. He stood up and

167

continued on up the stairs towards me and passed directly in front of me with slow measured steps, head bowed. We were less than two feet apart in that narrow passage way. Not a word passed between us. As I always facetiously say, whenever I share this encounter, he did not even have the manners to say, 'Good Morning'.

The police were called and they responded immediately. Thank God for the ministry of our policemen and women! But the 'midnight intruder' had made good his escape and left behind, as evidence of the reality of his intrusion, a lone footprint on the little roof upon which he had stepped, as he fled. The missing details to assuage your curiosity are documented for future reading.

What is clear to me is that God speaks to us in language that we can understand. If I were an architect, or maybe a mechanic, God would have used something from my profession to enlighten me. As an English teacher for the past thirty four years, having started at the age of 21, God knew that I would understand the concept of prolepsis. He knew that I would correctly interpret the coded message which I would need for the long haul.

The concept of prolepsis I would have taught many years earlier, when I was teaching Shakespeare's Romeo and Juliet to one of the myriad of fifth form classes I have had over the years. Very simply, it is a device where the writer uses one incident to point forward symbolically to a future event. It is a kind of foreshadowing. Via that incident God clearly and unequivocally revealed to my heart that the same way that the man had entered my physical house, if anything went awry with my physical body, I would have His help and protection.

Even now as I type this on December 26, 2013, I can look behind me (and I did) to see the same stairs and the same wall against which I propped as the midnight prowler passed me without touching a hair on my head on December 1, 2003. Do the Maths! He met a force that crippled Him. No weapon formed against us shall prosper! None!

The other message that connected with the intruder incident came in my visit to the naturopathic practitioner. At that time it was Dr. David Homer. At that visit, I learnt that the uterus was only a symptom. He said we needed to get to the root. He never gave me a diagnosis, to this point no doctor ever has. But God told me that I would go through the valley of the shadow of death *standing up*. I believe that God meant what He said and He knew I would need a very strong, radical and bull terrier faith to get me through. God knew that I did not have it, but He would have to develop it in me.

Back to the visit, from reading the fine print of Dr. Homer's report after the examination of my blood, I inferred that it was indeed a grave situation... pun on the word *grave*. Angels can be sent to protect us but we have protection in the Word of God. The Word is rendered impotent for the one who does not believe it. Indeed, 'It is no secret what God can do, what He has done for others He can do for you'. Just believe the promises in the Word!

****

A Slim Ox

—— ⚜ ——

The LORD God is my strength – He will make my feet like those of a deer, equipping me to tread on my mountain heights. Habakkuk 3:19 ISV

God arms me with strength and He makes my way perfect. Psalm 18:32 NLT

There are different kinds of strengths - physical, moral, emotional and spiritual. I would say that my journey has been characterized by a strength which is supernatural. It is God who arms us with strength and His strength is perfect. In fact, in Him is *everlasting* strength, so we need not have an undulating experience. (See Isaiah 26:4)

When God pours His strength into us, we are equipped to accomplish feats which would otherwise be impossible. (See Psalm 18:34) God's strength in my journey has been manifested in many different ways. I am slim but my strength in the gym amazes even me. I still love working with the weights and can attest to the fact that my investment of time and money in exercising has not been wasted.

The physical strength to keep up with all my activities, to my mind, is phenomenal. In all this time, except for two or three weeks of 'sick leave' in May 2004, I have kept up an excellent attendance at school. Some terms I have not even been absent a single day. I placed the words sick leave in inverted commas simply because it was not as if I was incapacitated and at death's door. Not at all! (Some may have feared for me...) I was experiencing some discomfort which started at school a Friday. The next day, Sabbath, I had two speaking engagements both of which I kept, despite some discomfort. The one in the evening, the title as given to me, was, "The Valley of Death". How ironic!

On Sunday, I went to the doctor for pain killers. I never once doubted God's direction. After giving me his views, Dr. X wrote the prescription and offered me time off to rest. Based on what He told me, I responded by telling him that he would come to a praise service or my funeral.

On my return to the car, the Holy Spirit spoke clearly to me with the words: 'None of what he said came from Us.' Dr X. questioned my ability to hear from God. That comment was outside the ambit of his medical views. Actually, I have had two praise services during this time. The first one was in 2004 and many of my colleagues were in attendance and the second was to celebrate my 50th birthday.

With the time off from school though, I was able to correct all my exam papers at home, as I gratefully rested in bed. (All the details, some quite humorous, are documented in the main publication.)

As it relates to the strength to keep going, I must tell you about Mum's health journey, which is interwoven with mine. Over the last two years my Mum has been hospitalized over twenty times. Then in 2012, she was in the hospital for three months which culminated in an above knee amputation. I have kept pace with her and she is doing very well!

I kept also kept up with school and all my household activities. Yes, there were times I felt physically exhausted as I made that daily trek right up to the 'A' floor to visit my Mum. But God poured His strength into me and kept me going. Even now with her amputation and the changes which have come about, God is still pouring His strength into this little slender frame. God *never* gives you more than you can bear!! I can attest to that. With any increase in load, His grace certainly outstrips it. It is always sufficient!!!

One may have physical strength but be emotionally weak. A change in health can take its emotional toll. A very strong faith in God and an unswerving belief in such promises as found in Romans 8:28 and Jeremiah 29:11 can serve as a bulwark against anxiety and worry. That emotional strength to remain very strong in God, not questioning His purposes, but simply going with the flow of His plan has never abated in my life.

My spiritual strength during this time has grown as I have absorbed the Word of God. Personalizing and believing the promises can infuse tremendous strength. The Word becomes nourishment to the soul. Left to ourselves we are absolute weaklings. But we are admonished to be strong in the Lord and in the power of *His* might, not ours. The real strength is the one in the inner man: soul strength! *That is where it counts.* (See Ephesians 3:14-19)

****

A Life Purposefully Lived

---·◦❋◦·---

Precious in the sight of the LORD is the death of his saints. Psalm 116:15

For I know that my redeemer liveth, and that he shall stand at the latter day upon the earth: And though after my skin worms destroy this body, yet in my flesh shall I see God. Job 19:25 & 26

I remember reading where a writer said she was scurrying to get a publication completed, not realizing that God had designed that she must go through something first. In the midst of preparing this publication, God called me to go through the valley of death with my mother. It was not a devastating, and frightening experience, but one of peace and calm.

How do I feel? Am I in deep mourning and breaking down with depression? No! I obviously loved and will miss my Mum very much. But, my focus is on celebrating my mother's life and her stellar achievements. She has truly left her family and friends a legacy. You may view a wonderful power point presentation on YouTube at: http://www.youtube.com/watch.

Allow me to share with you, some snippets of the tribute I paid to my Mum at her celebratory service:

"My mother lived the Word of God. She understood the depth of Romans 8:28 that '...*all things worked together for good to those who loved God...*' She experienced the reality of 2 Timothy 1:7: *God has not given us a spirit of fear, but of love, power and a sound mind.* Because she believed and accepted the truth of Isaiah 43:2, and was not prepared to use her humanity as a crutch, she knew that she would have God's presence as she walked through the waters and that through the fire she would not be burnt.

My Mum obviously knew how to access the secret place of the Most High ... Psalm 91:1 *'He that dwelleth in the secret place of the most high shall abide under the shadow of the Almighty.'* Paradoxically, that secret place is very accessible, yet few find it. It cannot be bought by money, education, church membership, not even religion, pursued as a form. Nothing else but a deep, abiding and intimate relationship with God will put us there. My mother lived in that secret place because she abandoned herself to the will and purposes of God, never fighting the will of God, but falling in line with a quiet and submissive spirit. The road less travelled is the road to that place!

My Mum was many things to me. She stood as a grand old oak tree against the backdrop of my entire life and supported me wholeheartedly in all my endeavours. She obviously had a great influence on me and I think that just a little of her faith, courage and trust in God must have rubbed off on me. As we say, 'the apple does not fall very far from the tree.'

The Bible tells us that for those who die in Christ, we do not need to mourn as those who have no hope. Everyone's circumstances of departure will be different. Mum was prepared and so, in essence, she prepared me. God has revealed to my spirit that I can cry, but I do not need to mourn. My crying has come and will come intermittently in 'bits and pieces'. My mood is one of celebration, I am celebrating the life my mother lived and the excellent legacy she has left me, her grandchildren, and all her other family and friends.

She lived for eight days after she collapsed. She was placed on a ventilator, and was heavily sedated. Though she could not respond verbally, she certainly communicated to us by the movements of her eye muscles. I was able to talk with her and tell her how much I loved and appreciated her and ask her forgiveness for 'sweating' some silly 'small stuff'.

As someone told me, my Mum was not snatched away by the enemy, but was called to a gentle rest by her Heavenly Father. It is at times like these that we must believe the Word of God. I believe that my Mum died in Christ and will be in the first resurrection.

> *Behold, I shew you a mystery; we shall not all sleep, but we shall all be changed, in a moment, in the twinkling of an eye, at the last trump: for the trumpet shall sound, and the dead shall be raised incorruptible, and we shall be changed. 1 Corinthians 15:51 & 52*

It is my personal belief that my mother's name was written in the Book of Life when she passed. I saw her demeanour in the Emergency Room before she collapsed. She was humming a tune before things really intensified. My Mum left me a legacy of a calm and firm trust in God. She knew her God and I witnessed that her God never left her, never forsook her but was with her to the very end.

As a devout Seventh-day Adventist, she believed in the 'Blessed Hope' and was blessed by God to have had that belief, deepened and strengthened in a dream, which He gave her last year when we really wondered if she would have survived... but she did. My Mum lovingly prepared me for the inevitable and my Daddy God told me from long ago that when that time arrived, He would be with me. He is a Man of His word!!!

In 2009, my Mum wrote me a very touching letter where she demonstrated to me her unconquerable faith and trust in God. What she predicted certainly came to pass. That will explain why I cannot be all depressed and downtrodden, even though my Mum has gone. It's really not a 'Goodbye' but more a 'Goodnight'. My Mum was in and out of the hospital some twenty-three or twenty-four times over a two year period. She could have gone any of those times, but she always came back to us. She was very conscious that a day would come when she would not return home with me. Here is an excerpt from the letter written to me in September 29, 2009 while she was in the hospital:

My Darling Daughter,

Writing is not my passion, but there is so much love, gratitude etc, etc bubbling up in me for you that I must let some boil over to wash over you. You are such a marvellous person, (I commented that my mother was obviously biased) everything I prayed for you at your birth, God has answered and so much more! I don't deserve you, but then I don't deserve all the things He has done for me...

I am sure that these latest episodes brought home to you the reality of my mortality, they did for me as well; but I had no fear, because I could feel God's presence with me. I know that when it does come, God will make you strong and I am assured that you will have good support from the Church family.

Alleluia! God has just answered another prayer. I am coming home. Praise God! See you soon. Mummy"

End of quoted tribute.

I cannot seem to be in deep mourning and celebrate a life well lived all at the same time. The old traditional Bajan expression of grief where you are expected to 'bawl out': '*Wah law* muh *mudda dead*' and then attempt to fling yourself in the grave is not part of my grieving scenario.

I do not intend to be insensitive to those who must express their grief in such ways, but that is not my way, because of the circumstances of Mum's departure and the life she lived. At the graveside, I climbed up on the little mound of dirt surrounding the grave and requested to be allowed to pray. It was with a firm, steady voice that I offered a prayer of thanksgiving for my mother's life and for the assurance in God's word that she will live again. I can see her again, if I am faithful.

That prayer was not an impulse of moment. From at home, I had written my desires in my prayer journal. I asked God to give me the strength to pray at my Mum's graveside in the same way He had strengthened to pray at her bedside as a number of us surrounded her lifeless but still warm body. I was somewhat emotional then but at the graveside there was no crying. I felt very confident in the strength of God.

The graveside, as we know, is usually the most difficult and heart wrenching part of a funeral service. God honoured my Mum's confidence that I would be strong. When the time came for placing the wreaths on the grave, I placed mine. The funeral director, E. Pamela Small, commented: "You are really strong." I corrected her and told her that I have no strength of my own; my strength is really all in God.

In going through my Mum's personal effects and her tons of books, I found her **Purpose Driven Life** prayer journal which she started in 2005. You may remember the very popular book by Rick Warren *The Purpose Driven Life*. On the page designed for you to write your responses, my Mum wrote, and this is over eight years ago:

> *I want my name to be in the Book of Remembrance in Heaven. No one is remembered on earth forever. Some family member or friend may establish a scholarship or special day in a person's name, or the person may do it and then die. But do we really remember them? God has a number of His own unsung heroes to whom He will say: 'Come ye blessed of my Father...' I know my purpose is to be among that number and by God's grace in faith, I will.*

I cannot but be astounded by the dramatic irony of this statement written by my Mum in 2005, and discovered by me, in June 2013, *after her passing*. Only God knew what would have worked out and that we would in fact now be planning to establish a scholarship fund in her name. Thanks to Dr. Andrew Harewood and Pastor Winston Cooke who both made the suggestion that we should think about starting a fund.

It is very clear to me that my Mum knew her purpose on this earth and she lived it! She may be an unsung hero to many but those of us who truly knew her, can appreciate the legacy of faith and trust in God which she has bequeathed to us.

My mother is irreplaceable in her love and support of me. I have had several 'hit home' moments and the tears have trickled. The last was yesterday at the Gymnasium, June 8, 2013, where we had a national service in celebration of the 'Festival of The Laity'. This was the first time I was going there without her in her wheelchair. I marked the spot where she would have been seated and reflected that she would never be there again. Yes, I cried quietly and surreptitiously wiped the tears away.

But my God has assured me, in my heart, that He is better to me than a thousand mothers. I look forward to seeing my Mum again. She looked so regal and majestic in her casket. I could think of no better way to end my tribute at the service than by saying:"

> *Knowing my mother, she will spring out of that grave on resurrection morning triumphantly shouting: "Hallelujah! I got muh two feet and they are real. Check me out!*

****

Standing left to right: Nola, Debbie-Ann, Dereka-Lynn and Andy. Sitting: Brandon (Donna –Lee's husband) Pauline (holding Baby Julian Hargrett) and Donna - Lee.

Perennial Rejoicing

---•❀•---

Although the fig tree shall not blossom, neither shall fruit be in the vines; the labour of the olive shall fail, and the fields shall yield no meat; the flock shall be cut off from the fold, and there shall be no herd in the stalls: Yet I will rejoice in the LORD, I will joy in the God of my salvation. Habakkuk 3: 17 & 18

These verses challenge us all to a level of faith which is not the 'run of the mill' kind. Even though the fig tree does not blossom, nor is there fruit on the vines, the person who trusts God can still rejoice. Our rejoicing is not generated by circumstances but by our unwavering confidence that God who needs no counsellor, knows just what He is doing.

This rejoicing which bubbles up from the inside causes one to say: 'I am magnificently blessed.' To have a 'But if not' faith like the Hebrew boys is most likely the road less travelled. The group KUTLESS addresses that issue very creatively in the lyrics of a song where we are reminded that God will always be good even if things do not turn out just the way we expected.

As the lyrics state:

Even if the healing doesn't come
And life falls apart

And dreams are still undone
You are God You are good...

Indeed, God's ways are above our finite understanding at times. The lyrics of the song correctly encourage us to put our trust then in the character of God, which is in fact unchangeable. He will always be a God of love, because that is His nature.

When all is said and done the Christian must be able to say: 'Though he slay me, yet I will trust Him.' This does not contradict in any wise our belief that our God is a God of the impossible and can and will do the impossible in rewarding radical faith. But if not...

The Christian's position should never be to force God's hand but to submit to His plan. Some folk throw in the towel when their figs trees don't blossom or no fruit is on the vine. In fact, some even throw the towel *at God* in a rage and stomp away from the blessing which awaited them...just around the corner.

The text quoted above from Habakkuk has an interesting connection with Haggai 2:19 which says: "Is the seed yet in the barn? Yea, as yet the vine, and the fig tree, and the pomegranate, and the olive tree, hath not brought forth: from this day will I bless *You*."

As we apply the text to our circumstances, whatever they may be, God is saying to us that even if it looks, figuratively speaking, like the vine and the olive have not yet brought forth... "Do not give up, I will bless you." Each of us may find some occasion in our life's journey to apply that text to our experiences. By the way, knowing the Word theoretically is one level, but the level which transcends that and makes the telling difference is its application. The Holy Spirit is on hand to help with that process.

Nola Estwick

I figured that by the end of my writing journey, I would be closer to a butter ball turkey but hey no... I have to be content to be a slim ox. The Biblical heroes, men and women, did not throw in the towel. They persevered! Shall we follow in the excellence of their footsteps?

****

The Faithfulness of God

---•❃•---

Your love, O LORD, reaches to the heavens, your faithfulness to the skies. Your righteousness is like the mighty mountains, your justice like the great deep. O LORD, you preserve both man and beast. **Psalm 36:5-6 NIV**

I do not hide your righteousness in my heart; I speak of your faithfulness and salvation. I do not conceal your love and your truth from the great assembly. **Psalm 40:10 NIV**

The quality I love most about God is His faithfulness. The Bible extols this indispensable aspect of His wonderful nature. We are blessed when we personally experience His faithfulness. When we have tasted and seen that God is good, why, we can hardly be quiet. We have to shout out ...loudly!

With the passing of my Mum, I have done much thinking and reflecting and God has taken me back to the early days of my life to show me that even in my mother's womb, I was indeed blessed by His faithfulness. I have this private way of describing myself as 'Pauline's little bastard child' who has become God's adopted daughter. Yes, the term *bastard* carries with it such negative connotations. However, we do not control the circumstances of our birth.

Thankfully, our Heavenly Father runs an adoption agency and all who want to be adopted can be adopted. Once adopted, our Heavenly Father is faithful in chastising or correcting His children for their own good. Ironically enough, in the spiritual scheme of things the ones who do not understand or rebel against God's corrections are actually the ones who are the *real* bastards.

> *For whom the Lord loveth he chasteneth, and scourgeth every son whom he receiveth. If ye endure chastening, God dealeth with you as with sons; for what son is he whom the father chasteneth not? But if ye be without chastisement, whereof all are partakers, then are ye bastards, and not sons.*
> Hebrews 12:6-8 King James Version

God is always faithful and the hallmark of any true friend is one who, though he/she will continue to love you, will also point out the error of your ways. Such friendships may be rare. When we *truly* enter into a friendship with God, He must in love show us the error of our ways and help us to make amends by His grace.

As I reviewed my Mum's Purpose Driven Life prayer journal, I see her acknowledging that though the circumstances of my birth were not God's ideal, yet I was not an accident. By man's calculation and harsh judgment, I was, but by God's strategic planning, no! I am my mother's only child and she loved me very much. She recounts her feelings about those difficult days, as a teenager, when I came on the scene. The social climate was very different from what it is now.

Based on Mummy's reflective thoughts which she documented, I could see that God's hand was with her, guiding her to persevere and not to succumb to negative thoughts and actions. Though unplanned, my birth was not a mistake. This is what my Mum wrote:

My thinking about the circumstances of Nola's birth is confirmed. It was an act of God. Only God is able to create someone so beautiful from a sinful action. Praise God!

(My Mum wore rose coloured glasses.) The journal page on which she wrote is captioned *You Are Not An Accident* and Mum's comment is written after Pastor Warren says:

Long before you were conceived by your parents, you were conceived in the mind of God. It is not fate, nor chance, nor luck, nor coincidence that you are breathing at this very moment. You are alive because God wanted to create you.

God has been tremendously faithful to my Mum and to me. He blessed my mother with three lovely, talented and beautiful granddaughters and an adorable grandson. Praise God that He held my Mum firm and strong even when she did not really know Him. He is faithful even when we do not acknowledge His faithfulness because we do not know that He is the one helping us out.

What are we to do though when we know *for sure* that He has been faithful to us? Well, I cannot help but join with the Psalmist David who declares:

I will extol thee, my God, O king; and I will bless thy name forever and ever. Every day will I bless thee; and I will praise thy name forever and ever. Great is the LORD, and greatly to be praised; and his greatness is unsearchable. Psalm 145:1-3

Simply revel in the entire chapter! Talk about the richness of the Word!

Since God has been so unflinchingly faithful to me, I do not want it to be a one-sided affair. Is God to dig around me and mulch me and give me manure and then when He comes to find fruit commensurate with His faithful care, all He finds is some leaves? (See Luke 6:6-9 to pick up the analogy) No!! There must be returns from my life for His magnanimous investment in me from my very birth!

Does this sound like boasting? If all of us started to really praise God for His mercy and faithfulness to us, the climate of the church would be different. We will all boast about something. For some, it will be their riches (See Psalm 49:6). Others may boast of their church affiliation while others boast of their achievements in life. But the Word of God admonishes us to boast *in God* all the day long. (See Psalm 94:4) The Psalmist declares: *My soul shall make her boast in the Lord.* (Psalm 34:2)

God's faithfulness to me in my life's entire journey, coupled with the example of faith I saw in my mother to her very end, inspires me to live as faithfully as she did. God's faithfulness reaches to the Heavens. It is like the sea, inexhaustible. Get your gear; we are heading out into its depths!!

****

God's Refreshment

---•❊•---

I will be like the dew to Israel; he shall blossom like the lily; he shall take root like the trees of Lebanon; his shoots shall spread out; his beauty shall be like the olive, and his fragrance like Lebanon. ESV

God has truly been refreshing me. I was reminded of how God can refresh in unusual ways when I reflected on an experience Elijah had. Elijah had been on a mission for God when the epitome of wickedness, Jezebel, threatened his life. As we say in Bajan parlance, he 'tek off' and ran like the wind from her fury.

You may read the entire account in 1 Kings 19. It was a long journey and poor Elijah was absolutely fagged out. He even wanted to die. His tiredness was not only physical but also emotional. He felt that he had had enough. God understood, as He always does, and sent an angel with some food for Elijah. It was simple fare: bread and water. No, he was not given macaroni pie and a big chicken leg. On that simple meal Elijah ran on for forty days and nights. That is simply amazing.

I think of my journey and the kind of food which has given me strength and stamina. My diet has been quite simple actually, totally vegan and practically all raw. I remember in the gym some time ago 'John' came and told me that I needed to eat some chicken, yet he was quite amazed at my strength. There are several books on raw food energy which you could possibly check out.

Besides the energy that comes from *living* foods, God has energized and refreshed me in many different ways. It seems as though He has placed refuelling stations all along my pathway. The first refuelling and refreshing station is in the morning when I have my quiet time. He feeds me with the finest of wheat and the best of honey from the rock. (See Psalm 81:16) What He serves is always fresh and appealing. There are always new perspectives to be gained!!!

On the strength of God's continual refreshment, I have kept running that race which is set before me. Such a race demands more than natural energy. It requires supernatural stamina, especially when it becomes a marathon.

Yet, on any long journey one can become physically exhausted. Elijah became physically exhausted which is not to be confused with spiritual weakness. In my journey I have been very busy, keeping up at times with many different things. As women, we can at times expend quite a lot of energy in the various roles we are called upon to play. This can take its toll.

One of my busiest times, when I know for sure God kept me together, was those eight days of my Mum's hospitalization for her final stint in that institution. I did not know how physically exhausted I was until I nearly fainted at Mum's bedside one Friday evening. A very attentive and concerned nurse was insistent that I should go to see a doctor in casualty. She knew my Mum and was aware of her frequent hospital visits.

She said: "You have been doing a lot of running up and down with your Mum; you need to look after yourself."

Well, the horrible feeling passed and I was wise enough not to drive myself back home. The next day, Sabbath, I remained at home and rested, well kept quiet, though I found myself writing about my experiences with Mum. That was when 'the call' came. I instinctively knew that it was all over. It came, not as a thunder bolt, but more as a message quietly relayed to an inner part of me that had been prepared to receive it. I was not there in those final moments as I had desired.

Even with Mum's passing and my going through that entire unprecedented episode, God was a tremendous tower of strength, refreshing me constantly so that I was able to make the preparations for the funeral with very little stress and still function at school, without taking any special doctor's leave. In fact, on one of my visits to the funeral home, Mum's body arrived while we were there doing our business. I asked the funeral director if I could go and see her. She asked if I was sure I could manage. I did manage, very well indeed. Mum was at peace and by God's grace so was I. Seeing her did not stress me out.

God surely knows how to be like dew to His children in their time of need. Hosea 14:5 & 6 say:

I will be like the dew to Israel; he shall blossom like the lily; he shall take root like the trees of Lebanon; his shoots shall spread out; his beauty shall be like the olive, and his fragrance like Lebanon. ESV

What a very loving, caring, kind, sensitive and compassionate God we have as our Heavenly Dad. He knows how to refresh and rejuvenate us, so that whatever happens, we need never become dried out because He is constantly refreshing us with His Heavenly dew.

****

189

Smiling At the Storm

---·◈·---

The disciples went and woke him, saying,
"Master, Master, we're going to drown!" He
got up and rebuked the wind and the raging
waters; the storm subsided, and all was calm.
Luke 8:24 NIV

Two! Three! Let's go: 'With Jesus in the vessel we can smile at the storm.... smile at the storm... as we go sailing on!' Great song!

However, have you been able to smile at and through your storms? Another nice little ditty which we sing with great gusto, as we sail on! But, what about when we actually navigate the seas of life and are confronted by storms?

The apostle Paul found himself in the midst of a fierce storm recorded in Acts Chapter 27. His storm is described thus: And when neither sun nor stars in many days appeared, and no small tempest lay on us, all hope that we should be saved was then taken away. (Acts 27:20) Paul's response to this literal storm is replete with lessons for us as we face the storms of life. (Please read the entire account in Acts 27)

Paul was confident that he belonged to God and was God's servant. We also need to be confident of who we are in God. Paul knew that he knew. We must know, that we know, that we know! This has nothing whatsoever to do with arrogance but more so with confidence in a God we have personally met as our Heavenly Father, our Daddy God, who will wrap His arms securely around us and take us through the storms of life.

Paul spoke encouragingly to the terrified men. His confidence was based on what the angel who visited him had told him. With strong words of assurance he said: 'So keep up your courage, men, for I have faith in God that it will happen just as he told me.' (Acts 27:25) Whatever kind of storm we face in life, we must have the assurance that we can get through it based on what our Heavenly Dad has told us. Paul knew the purpose of his life had not been fully met, so he could not die in the storm. But of course he died later, having completed his course.

Another interesting lesson about storms and how we face them can be gleaned from the Biblical narrative where the disciples battled a storm while Jesus slept peacefully. (See Matthew Chapter 8) When Jesus awoke to His disciples' cries, He chided them for their lack of faith: And he saith unto them, Why are ye fearful, O ye of little faith? Then he arose, and rebuked the winds and the sea; and there was a great calm. Matthew 8:26

The disciples had apparently forgotten that Jesus was in the boat with them and only at the point where they were at the end of their resources, did they seek His help. I have never for a moment forgotten that Jesus is in my boat.

As long as Jesus, the Creator of Heaven and earth, is on board with us and we are in His boat, we need not be terrorized by the storms of life. We are in His boat, in the sense of being in an abiding intimate relationship with Him.

Acting, as always, in our best interest, He will do one of two things... either He will calm the storm or calm us. Whatever in Divine wisdom, He chooses to do, we can smile, a genuine smile, and say: 'Even in the storm I am magnificently blessed!'

****

Will it be sand or rock?

———— ·◈· ————

Therefore everyone who hears these words of mine and puts them into practice is like a wise man who built his house on the rock. The rain came down, the streams rose, and the winds blew and beat against that house; yet it did not fall, because it had its foundation on the rock. Matthew 7: 24 & 25 NIV

Though we do not consciously think about it, we are all building spiritual houses. The metaphor of building a storm resistant house is directly connected in these texts with hearing and obeying the Word of God. We may all hear the Word, and we do so in a myriad of ways. By the way, I would very highly recommend *The Bible Experience* for a par excellent rendering of a dramatized reading of the Bible. I am hooked on it even while in the gym. *Acting* on the Word however, allowing it to inform your lifestyle, and influence your decisions is the 'unlocking' step beyond merely hearing.

There is much depth of meaning in the words: '...it had its foundation on the rock'. An interesting thing about a foundation is that once it is laid, you do not really see it and you cannot know its strength ... until a storm comes. This is true for both the physical house and the spiritual house. A pretty and impressive looking house on a weak foundation will totter.

In the spiritual realm, our foundation is laid once we have really met Jesus and we remain in a committed, loving and non-legalistic relationship with Him. When I was twenty three years I made a commitment of my life to a God I really met for the first time. A critical element of building a foundation with God is spending time with Him. Having my 'quiet time' or 'devotional time' has always been very important to me. A devotional writer called Andrew Murray has excellent spiritual literature on nurturing that quiet time with God.

It is in my early morning quiet time that I do most of my reading, studying, meditating and praying. Though it is an indispensable part of my lifestyle, it is not ritualistic, it's not an, 'I got to do it' kind of thing because God won't be happy with me. Not at all!! These are moments I absolutely love and enjoy to the max. They are my special moments with God...my courting time.

My husband would attest to the fact that over the thirty two years of our marriage, you would never find me in bed at six o'clock, not even at five. I am up and gone! My three children were born and met their Mum having her quiet time. On an occasion Donna-Lee, as a little toddler, sought me out very early, finding me bent over praying, she simply climbed on my back and went fast asleep. Breast feeding was often done in the midst of my quiet time. A mother has to learn how to multi-task!

You can be in church and never have *really* met God. You can also be a member of a church and the concept of a quiet time is foreign to you. Some folk may just awake, say a little obligatory pray and rush into the day. At night, they may yawn a prayer at God and fall fast asleep. Such a situation continued on with for years cannot build a strong spiritual house. It's a sure way to construct a weak spiritual foundation.

Spending *quality time* with God is what enables you to get to know Him better and better and to be able to discern His voice. It was at age twenty three that I started to build my spiritual house, though I did not conceive of it as that. I always loved reading and many spiritual writers have helped to shape me and enabled me to dig a deep foundation in God.

A book which influenced me in a telling way and contributed greatly to my spiritual growth was the book *Desire of The Ages* by Ellen G. White. This outstanding piece of spiritual literature contributed to my conversion experience in 1980, along with Morris Venden's commentary *Faith That Works*. (I read that Pastor Venden, absolutely one of my favourite spiritual writers, died on February 10, 2013. May his works continue to bless others.) His insightful commentary and the *Desire of The Ages* took me to the level of applying spiritual truths to my life. The knowledge has served me in good stead.

The material with which you construct your spiritual foundation may not be seen. But if you cheat, you will only cheat yourself. The Word of God encourages us to build with material which can withstand pressure. (See 1 Corinthians 3: 12-15) The fire and storm will test our architectural structure. If we have built merely on church membership and position, and not on Jesus as our rock, it will be seen. The principle of reaping and sowing is also relevant here. You cannot construct a sturdy house on a weak and faulty foundation. You will reap what you have sown.

Two houses may look alike in terms of their outward structure, but the storm makes the difference. The house built on sand cannot withstand the onslaught of a change in weather. Those who have built on sand are those who hear the Word but *do not put it into practice*. God's Word has power but the power is not merely in hearing. *We must "do the Word."*

****

God's Favourite

———————•●❀●•———————

Keep me as the apple of Your eye; hide me in the shadow of Your wings. Psalm 17:8

See, I have engraved you on the palms of my hands; your walls are ever before me. Isaiah 49:16 NIV

I know that I am God's favourite. So are you!! I know that God had His eye on me even before I was born. He marked me out to do something special for Him. The conviction that I was very special to God dawned on me in my very early twenties. That unprecedented consciousness of being individually loved by God has never left me.

My first baptism was at age of ten. At that time, I certainly did not understand the implications of that major decision. With the passage of the years and my growth in a friendship with God, I wanted to seal my life to be lived forever with Him. I chose to be baptized a second time in my forties, when I could say my vows intelligently, knowing that it would be until death do us part!

I have an entire letter called 'Birthday Testimony' addressing the issue of re-baptism. It was not done out of a fall from grace but from a burgeoning understanding of the fact that baptism is really a marriage and I wanted to say my vows when I could do so with a full understanding of the implications.

I have always said and felt that as I walk through my experiences with God, I would never want to put Him to shame, never sully His character, never disgrace the Family name and be a black sheep. I believe that if God tells me that He wants me to love Him as outlined in Deuteronomy 6:5 'Love the LORD your God with all your heart and with all your soul and with all your strength, then it must be possible.

Loving God is what makes all the difference in our Christian experience. We can either be motivated by a deep passionate love for Him or by a legalistic spirit. We are obeying simply out of duty, just like the older brother in the Parable of the Prodigal Son. Legalists, except they become converted, can never enter into a joyful, happy, excited, passionate relationship with God because they are very busy striving to please God in their own strength, doing the right things, maybe, but for all the wrong reasons.

Loving God enables you to view all of the events in your life in the light of Calvary, and it is what really opens up the gateway to a life of faith. Faith is always about how you live, not just what you say. Faith is not about how you feel. Feelings can always change. A mere emotional love of God may stop short there and not go on to include the intellect and the will.

Emotional lovers of God may enjoy a 'feel good' religion without engaging their wills in the matter of obedience. Therein lies the test! Loving God and trusting Him enables us to understand that all that God permits is for our good. All that touches us must first come through His hand, filtered and measured, as He takes into account our strength.

Years ago, one of my church sisters, Carmen, sent me a beautiful story taken from Streams in The Desert. She said that when she read it, she remembered me. The third woman in the story would have to be a woman after God's own heart. Her pathway would definitely be the road less travelled.

The story is based on the text: He will be silent in His love Zephaniah 3:17. The gist of the story is that a woman dreamt that she praying with three other women. Jesus approached the three women but treated all of the very differently. He gave much of His attention to the first woman. The second woman He touched and gave her a look of approval. However, the third woman He totally ignored, it appeared to the lady who was dreaming. She surmised that Jesus did not love that one as much as He loved the two other women.

Jesus corrected her false assumptions, explaining that the two women He seemed to have favoured above the third one, needed all that He did for them. But of the third woman in the story this is what Jesus said:

> *The third, whom I seemed not to notice and even neglect has faith and love of the finest quality and her, I am training by quick and drastic processes for the highest and holiest service. She knows me so intimately and trusts me so utterly that she is independent of words or look or any outward intimation of my approval.*
>
> *She is not dismayed nor discouraged by any circumstance through which I have arranged that she shall pass. She trusts Me when sense and reason and every finer instinct of the natural heart would rebel because she knows that I am working in her for eternity, and that what I do, though she knows not the explanation now, she shall understand hereafter.*

'Awesome indeed! Can we rise to the challenge and travel the road... less travelled?

If you have the book *Streams in The Desert* you may find the story in the February 9 reading in Volume 1, or in Volume 2, the reading for January 8. This book is such an excellent book, you should consider purchasing one or access the readings on the internet.

****

What in the World am I Doing Here?

Wherefore should the heathen say, Where is now their God? Psalm 115:2

He says, "Be still, and know that I am God I will be exalted among the nations. I will be exalted in the earth. Psalm 46:10

Everyone who is called by my name, whom I created for my glory, whom I formed and made. Isaiah 43:7 NIV

Having a sense that God created us for a purpose can add a distinct supernatural dimension to our lives. Certainly, the raison d'etre for our presence on this earth, our very life, is more than what the cynical Macbeth asserts: "Life's but a walking shadow, a poor player that struts and frets his hour upon the stage and then is heard no more: it is a tale told by an idiot, full of sound and fury, signifying nothing." (Macbeth Act 5 Scene 5)

Cynicism can creep into anybody's life, even the lives of Christians, unless they are is fortified with an unshakable confidence that God created them for a specific purpose. That specific purpose is to bring glory to God. God's glory is really His character. When Moses asked to see God's glory, God showed Moses Himself. He told Moses what He was really like.

Exodus 33:18 & 19: Then Moses said, "Now show me your glory. And the LORD said, "I will cause all my goodness to pass in front of you, and I will proclaim my name, the LORD, in your presence. I will have mercy on whom I will have mercy, and I will have compassion on whom I will have compassion.

Someone noted that:

> *If we don't know His (God's) goal and our lives are not in alignment with it, then we will find ourselves at cross purposes with God. It is a fearful thing to be at cross purposes with your Maker! But on the other hand, nothing inspires courage and endurance and pluck for daily living like knowing the purpose of God and feeling yourself wholeheartedly in harmony with it.*

(See: http://www.desiringgod.org/resource-library/sermons/god-created-us-for-his-glory)

Very well said! I believe that even before I was born, God designed my life and part of it was the publication which will follow this mini one. An awesome, and I mean awesome, chapter for you to sink your teeth in is found in the book *God Sent a Man*. The chapter is entitled: "To Egypt and Slavery".

It is what we *believe* in the depths of our souls that will bring radiance to our lives. The joy of the Lord has to be our strength when we believe what God tells us. Here is the quotation:

> *There is a definite life plan, divine shaped for every human being. Each of us is meant to do some exact thing and the circumstances of our lives are designed to prepare us for its accomplishment. The true significance and glory of our lives will be the*

doing of the thing that God has marked out for us.[50]
This is very powerful!

Do you know what God has marked out for you to do? I do. I spare no pains in telling my three daughters that God has a specific plan for their lives. I have constantly reinforced that they must not make up their own plan but seek to find out what God's plan is. That will be the winning plan. Granted, it may involve some disappointments along the way but God's plan, when it all comes together is always perfect.

My daughter Debbie-Ann who recently took up the position of Director of Communications at our Seventh-day Adventist University, USC, in Trinidad knows most assuredly that being there is part of God's plan for her life. The path leading there was not paved with gold. But everything came together with divine precision with the providential closing and opening of doors. God is a strategic planner and I'm glad that His plan for my life is one based on love and divine wisdom.

So the question posed, 'What am I doing here?' is merely rhetorical for me. I know that I am...

****

---

[50] Carlyle B. Haynes, God Sent A Man, Review and Herald Publishing Association, Washington, DC 20039 (1962) p 51

Called For a Purpose

—————————•❖•—————————

The Lord will fulfill his purpose for me; your steadfast love, O Lord, endures forever. Do not forsake the work of your hands. Psalm 138:8 ESV

Do you hold to the Epicurean belief that you are here to simply 'eat, drink and be merry, for tomorrow we die'? Or do you sense that you were born for something special, something *only you* have been called to do? Are only ministers of the gospel called? While you ponder the questions placed on the table, this is what the deeply engaging and thought provoking spiritual writer Henry Blackaby asserts in his book *Called and Accountable:*

> *Unfortunately our 'Christian culture' has not always been thoroughly biblical. That is, as we have made a difference between clergy and lay people so we have made a difference between the specially called and the common believer. **All are called.** The differences lie not in whether we are called or not, but in the nature of the assignment we are given by God. But every believer is one who is called by God, for Him to be free to accomplish His purposes in them and through them.*[51]

---

[51] Henry T. Blackaby, *Called and Accountable*, New Hope Publishers, (2012) p 53

This concept of each believer having a specific assignment in his/her life's journey is reiterated by Carlyle B. Haynes in his book *God Sent a Man*. Using the story of Joseph as a basis for his comments, Haynes postulates that just as Joseph was sent, (see Genesis 45:8) so are we all.

He states: "What I would have you believe is that every man is sent from God. All persons born into this world are born with some purpose to fulfil, with a mission to accomplish." He further adds that "....All persons may have this consciousness of God's call, a sense of mission, of destiny."[52]

My reading makes it clear to me that not only the Biblical characters were called but modern day believers, spoken as of the called of God, chosen by God or set apart by God. These are also 'called'. Several texts allude to the idea 'a calling'. (See Romans 1:6, Ephesians 1:18 and 2 Thessalonians 1:11)

In October 2004, I was the focus of a very memorable and special occasion which I have called 'Nola's Heart Day'. It is vividly described in Prayer Letter # 11. It was when I was at the home of Miss Irisdene Samuel in Queens, New York that a mature spiritual sister, Polly Cornelius, uttered some strange pronouncements. Among the things she said, was that I was one of 'The Called'. Her concept was taken from Romans 8:28: "All things worked together for good to those who are *the* called according to the purpose of God".

She placed special emphasis on the definite article. Most of us in repeating the text do tend to unconsciously omit that 'the'. Is it of import? Maybe so, as it seems to zero in on a specific group of persons. That special group of persons is really *all believers*.

---

[52] Carlyle B. Haynes, *God Sent A Man*, Review and Herald Publishing Association, Washington, DC 20039 (1962) p 50

We are familiar with the expression, "Many are called but few are chosen". All people who attend church may not have this consciousness of a divine calling for their lives. Happy with their churchgoing experience and the meticulous execution of their church programmes, their thinking does not transcend to the higher sense of their purpose on this earth.

If we spend decades in church and miss the very raison d'être for our existence, that would truly be a tragedy. Living our purpose is bound up with our calling. There can be nothing vicarious about it. At its simplest level, we are called to live a beautiful life, not by our standards, but by God's.

In 2002, at the request of Dr. Andrew Harewood, I wrote a poem for an iconic lady, Mrs. Thelma Lora Winston Kibble. The family wanted a poem composed around the theme of a beautiful life to commemorate the journey of their loved one. I was laid hands upon suddenly, possibly unavoidably so, and I knew absolutely nothing about Mrs. Kibble, when Dr. Harewood made the request on the family's behalf.

I love writing and I joyfully jumped to the task. It was undoubtedly my Literary Friend, the Holy Spirit, who inspired the words of the poem entitled *A Beautiful Life*. Thankfully, the family loved the poem and included it in the funeral brochure as part of the tributes to their loved one. I learnt of Mrs. Kibble's stellar achievements as an educator and family person only *after* I received the funeral brochure. The poem was a perfect match, incredibly divinely orchestrated!

We are all called to live beautiful life. Such a life is not influenced by marital status, gender, race, religion, age or any of the other ways we may seek to categorize ourselves. A beautiful life, by God's measuring stick, is not a life of ostentation, which is lived to impress others and to curry favour and glory from man.

Instead, it is a life lived in the centre of God's will, whose sole purpose is to influence others for the Kingdom of God and to showcase the exquisite charms of God's wonderful nature. I aspire by God's grace to live what I penned for someone else:

A BEAUTIFUL LIFE ....

Is like a piece of tapestry into which God
has blended and interwoven the
colourful qualities of His own nature ....
Gentle, kindness, compassion and deep caring
Producing a canvas on which the Master Artist
Has inscribed His signature
A beautiful life pulsates and radiates with
The tenderness of God
Like the calm in the eye of the storm...
It knows that peace which passeth all understanding
In the midst of trial and perplexity calmly acknowledging
That God is a fortress wherein lies safety.
Touching, loving, healing, forgiving, nurturing and
selflessly giving until there is no more left......
And such a life she lived.....
A wonderfully sweet, wife, mother, grandmother,
sister, friend and confidante
She lived a life of hope and nurtured hope in others.
The lustre of her life shines beyond the grave in the
lives it has illuminated....even for a brief time.
A beautiful life.... never dies
For its memories are indelibly etched
In the minds of those it has succoured.
Our loved one, though departed, has left
us a treasure of inestimable price
The legacy of a BEAUTIFUL LIFE.
May she rest in peace until that great morning.
The End

Nola Estwick

Our real purpose in this world is to bless others by our lives, as
we respond to the called of servant hood.

****

Blessed With A Servant's Heart

—•❀•—

His lord said unto him, well done, thou good and faithful servant: thou has been faithful over a few things, I will make thee ruler over many things: enter thou into the joy of thy lord. Matthew 25:21

It is incredible, but true. In 1984, my fifth form students presented me with a lovely gift. Their wise choice was a lovely framed mirror with the inspirational words of a poem inscribed in letters of gold. It is the *only* gift from my students which has survived the many years of our moving from house to house. For the most part, it has decorated the walls of our various homes. Right now, I can see it while I do some indoor exercise on my trampoline.

I absolutely love the words of this inspirational poem and would like them to be reflective of my life. We are truly here to bless the lives of others. If, when our days are done, folk can genuinely say that we added to their lives, then we would have achieved a part of our life's purpose.

I wonder what led the students who bought that gift to select it. 'Nothing happens by chance', as we say. Knowing me, I guess my students figured that I would appreciate it. Something of a cosmetic nature would definitely not have been as enduring. I wonder which students made the choice. Maybe someday I will find out. May this prayer be reflective of our lives: The first four lines of the poem are quoted:

A Servant's Prayer:
Diana Kay Haerr

Give me a chance, oh Lord, I pray
To be used by You, somehow, today.
That in some manner I may find
A way to bless and enrich others' minds...

The poem in its entirety may be seen at the following site: http://www.straighttalkministry.com/blog/2010/11/30/Faithful-Servants.aspx

I have always said that it is not so much quantity that counts in the final analysis; it is really the *quality* of our lives. We should live our years in such a way as to bless and enrich the lives of others. If that enrichment has been to inspire someone to cut through all the religious red tape and doctrinal confusion to really meet and know God, then we would have lived a noble life. A hearty 'Thank You' to the students of the 1984 class! Your gift was not accidentally chosen. There was design in its choice.

****

Seeing With New Eyes

---·❀·---

My ears had heard of you but now my eyes
have seen you. Job 42:5 NIV

Job's experience brought him into a deeper relationship with
God. With spiritual eyes, born out of the crucible, he saw God
anew. How we view God, our concept of Him, His character,
will certainly influence how we travel through the storms life is
sure to bring us.

It's amazing how we may all have different perceptions of God
even though we all read the same Bible, or even attend the same
church. Our views of God are shaped by our experiences in life
and our perception of Him is influenced by what significant
others tell us and how they treat us. Our views are also shaped
by our religious teachings. False teachings do their deadly and
insidious work. I believe, as a young girl, I met *the real God* and
not a caricature. In a prayer letter called *Birthday Testimony* I
recount that 'epiphany'. My journey inspired me to write the
following poem:

In God's Darkroom

Slowly the image developed and took form
I glimpsed God....
Moses was correct!
Opening the aperture of my mind

I caught Him
It was a timed exposure
I've seen His face
In each lineament
I could trace expressions of tenderness
He has stamped His image on my soul
People have painted such horrible pictures of Him
I see His radiant smile and shining eyes
On our official wedding day
There were no flashing cameras
But my heart saw God's pleasure
At my boldness
In the darkroom of my life
I see a picture of a child
Climbing into Daddy's lap
Looking squarely in His face
Snap! Another picture is taken
I know I can never be mistaken
Will never be forsaken
No demon in hell
Can erase from the files of my mind
The image of a Dad so gracious and kind
One who carries me day by day
Down the valley
Through death's narrow alley
But, it is not a cul-de-sac
At the end of life's track
My God says:
Look at My face, read My lips
Not one of my promises I will let slip
You are not in the departure lounge of life
Destined for your final exit
Not a bit
Those who think so will catch a fit
Cause in this experience...is bare sixes we plan to hit!
You must paint My picture before your world

Let them see the hues of My character
The varied tints of My love
You needed the dark room to see Me better
You must now become My letter
To free my children who have been fettered
Snap!
You have seen My face
Now, as a spiritual artist go wild with colour
And paint with all the energies of your soul
My goodness and My power.

N.Estwick
Originally Written: December 2004
Refined and Polished May 6, 2006

****

Going *Through* Not Under.....

---·◦❀◦·---

Thou hast caused men to ride over our heads; we went through fire and through water: but thou broughtest us out into a wealthy place. Bless our God, O peoples! Give him a thunderous welcome! Didn't he set us on the road to life? Didn't he keep us out of the ditch? He trained us first, passed us like silver through refining fires, brought us into hardscrabble country, pushed us to our very limit, road-tested us inside and out, took us to hell and back; Finally he brought us to this well-watered place. Psalm 66: 8-12 (Message Bible)

Going through an experience with God as your shield, buckler, anchor or refuge, just to mention a few of the metaphors used to symbolize God's presence, could never be the same as travelling alone. It is God's intention to bring us eventually to that wealthy or well watered place. From such a position of abundance, we are able to share our spiritual wealth. We are strategically positioned to influence people to see God anew or to meet Him for the first time.

But how do you get through the fire and through the water, two potentially destructive forces, to that place of abundance? In Prayer Letter # 36, written July 2007, called *Going Through*,

I explored twenty ways we can avoid an aborted or disastrous journey. Here are two of the ways which were mentioned:

> *Bring God on board from the word go! If you attempt to go through without Him, it will be a miserable experience. What God intends you to learn, you will not learn, and in mercy, He may have to allow you to go through again. We must bring God 'on board' not cosmetically, but realistically. If He is really brought into our experience as manager, then we must allow Him to direct us and not vice versa.*

> *"Lavishly use the Word of God. Read it, assimilate it, and apply it to your situation. Any special promises that God has given to you, type them out and keep them with you or mount them in areas around the house where you are able to see them. Memorise the Word, so that you can bring it to mind quickly to counteract any darts from the enemy.* July 2007 (End of extracts).

I think that Prayer Letter 36 is a very practical hands-on approach to getting through any experience and we never know just how soon we will need such advice. The letter will be made available before the main publication is completed to anyone who desires to read the other eighteen road tested points which were made.

****

Going Through The Flood on Foot

For this shall every one that is godly pray unto thee in a time when thou mayest be found: surely in the floods of great waters they shall not come nigh unto him. Psalms 32:6

I sink in deep mire, where there is no standing: I am come into deep waters, where the floods overflow me. Psalms 69:2

He turned the sea into dry land: they went through the flood on foot: there did we rejoice in him. Psalms 66:6

The Lord sitteth upon the flood; yea, the Lord sitteth King forever. Psalms 29:10

If it's not a storm, then maybe it will be a flood. It was a very rainy Sunday as we set off to go to a luncheon. Approaching the familiar descent in a road known to flood with water, I had to make a quick decision. All I could see ahead of me was what looked like a flowing river. I decided to try another route. I made a quick right turn just before the descent. Ahead of me lay another more shallow descent, deceptively so.

"No, Mummy no, don't go down there. Stop Mummy! Stop!" came the plaintive wails of Dereka-Lynn as she sat in the back

214

assessing the situation. Ignoring her frantic entreaties, I advanced slowly into the water. I expected it to be a slight descent but... the car kept going down...and down... Little did I know that I had gone from the frying pan *into the fire!* The engine started to sputter and cough. I was now revving heavily, but to no avail. Suddenly the beleaguered engine coughed her last... and died. Silence.

We sat there momentarily, Dereka-Lynn, my Mum and I. What next? Water started seeping its way steadily into the car as the level kept rising. We were in a real slump. Death by drowning was not such a far-fetched idea. "Family of Three Drowned in The Bush Hall Area".

Dereka-Lynn by now was absolutely panic-stricken and her wailing turned into loud piteous bellowing. The birthday gift which had lain on the back seat was now literally afloat. We started to call loudly for help. Not a cricket stirred though there were houses around.

Finally, a lady came out right into all that murky water in her petticoat to assist us. She had been sleeping and I guess Dereka-Lynn's frantic screams awakened her. She lifted Dereka-Lynn through the car window. By now, the water was about half way up the side of the car. Having deposited Dereka-Lynn in her house, this kind lady returned and helped Mummy out. I finally opened my door and the water just gushed its way through even more.

To say we were like wet ducks would be an understatement. So much for Mummy Barrow's birthday luncheon!! As for the car, the engine collected much debris from the water which engulfed it and the Chefette cup found under the hood told the tale. Thankfully, the engine was not damaged and the seats were restored after a valet and ... we escaped drowning!!

To be suddenly engulfed by a flood of water could be quite frightening. When the metaphorical floods of life seek to wipe us out, the Word of God offers great encouragement. First of all, God sits on the floods! Wow! He is in control so there is no need to be panic-stricken. Secondly, when we pray to Him He can keep the floods at bay, 'the floods of great waters shall not come nigh unto him'. And, if we must go through a flood then God can cause us to go through the flood on foot.

However you look at it, God has it all worked out. Psalm 46 is a very powerful Psalm and we are reminded that though the waters roar and be troubled that we need not fear because God is *indeed* our refuge and strength... even on these 'dry weather' Barbadian roads!!

****

Shunning The Grim Reaper

Teach us to realize the brevity of life, so that we may grow in wisdom. Psalm 90:12 NLT

These all died in faith, not having received the promises, but having seen them afar off, and were persuaded of them. Hebrews 11:13

And they have conquered him by the blood of the Lamb and by the word of their testimony, for they loved not their lives even unto death. Revelation 12:11

Talking candidly about death is a bit of a taboo subject. Even though we all will acknowledge that in the midst of life, there is death, we still shy away from the subject, least of all, talking about our own demise. There is really no need to fear death since Jesus holds the keys and we cannot go to the grave without His permission. People may number our days for us but the Bible assures us that: "God is to us a God of deliverances; and to GOD the Lord belong escapes from death." Psalm 68:20 NASB

Yes, we do need to number our days and apply our hearts to wisdom. That text tells me that I am not immortal and that I have a certain number of days on this earth. Therefore, I need to live righteously and soberly. (See Titus 2:12 & 13) Someday we will all die, except we live until Jesus returns. It will be one or the other. But there is yet another option. We will either die in Christ or die in our sins. Some may sneer at this.

Eternal life however is not automatic. We cannot live as we like, do as we please, and then be ushered into Heaven. On these matters we need to be very clear. The pillars, on which we have built our lives, if false, will crumble as we face our life's end. We cannot afford to make any mistakes here.

Regrettably, some folk only think seriously about God when they become ill. They live life without any reference to God's purposes for them. However, the storms of life will challenge them to think of their Maker and their destiny. Thankfully, the loving God I have seen in action is right on hand with the assurance found in John 6:37. Even at the last minute some will come and will not be turned away. (See Matthew 20:1-16) What a loving and merciful God we serve!

However, we do not want to wait until the last minute, as it were. Our best option is to live *in Christ* and to live *for Him.* That is not some sanctimonious, holier than thou, reclusive, legalistic and starchy kind of living. Not at all! It really is an abundant, adventurous and exciting kind of life, where you are walking in God's will and executing all your divine appointments. What can beat that?

****

Imprisoned?

—•◦❀◦•—

.... And deliver them who through fear of death
were all their lifetime subject to bondage.
Hebrews 2:15

As already established, the subject of death is not 'teatime' talk. That grim reaper strikes terror in our quailing hearts. I remember an experience which occurred in 1998. Let me recapture it as succinctly as I can. I had a small growth, like a mole, on my torso, and the mole started to hurt after a while. On my *very first visit* to Dr. Q, he lost no time in informing me, in my view, in an insensitively callous and casual fashion: "Well, if it is a malignant melanoma, you will have about six months." He rocked back in his chair as if he had told me I had the flu.

I was totally shocked! 'A lil mole!' That threw me into such a state of panic. I immediately concluded the worst and by the time I reached school, it was a corpse who drove through the gates.

Dr.Q said they would have to do minor surgery and examine the tissue. I agreed to the procedure. The days leading to the procedure and the days following were days of much anxiety. To use Bajan parlance, "Uh had stomach burn and palpitations of de heart, de fear alone did enuff to kill muh." It was a nerve wracking time – an absolute reign of terror in my poor quailing heart.

One morning, soon after the procedure, while I was at home engaged in my quiet time, the Lord spoke. He revealed to me my blind spot. It came as a shock. I had queried within myself, how could I have a relationship with God and still be overwhelmed with such anxiety and trepidation. It just seemed incongruous to me, but I could find no explanation for the puzzling incongruity.

God offered one. The words embedded themselves in my consciousness as if someone had said them audibly to me: 'You do not trust Me.' Those words, quietly deposited in my spirit, could find no rebuttal. I had to admit to their accuracy. The mask was gently and not roughly lifted. I saw the truth. The gentleness of our Friend, the Holy Spirit!! He is the best Counsellor ever!

It was then that God gave me the mental image of the platform of faith. I was to stand in the middle of this platform. I was not to venture to the edge seeking to peek over because I could be dragged off. Sounds weird? God sometimes uses word pictures to teach us spiritual truths. That was a very deep one.

I was made aware that I simply did not understand what trusting God really meant. Now I know. Trust and fear simply cannot coexist. One will stifle the other. The results of the lab report came back and it was nothing. All was well. The feeling I had of dangling off the edge of a precipice abruptly ended with the phone call which apprised me of the lab report.

I feared death and that was really why I was in such a panic. It hit me recently that our carnal nature craves the easiest exit possible, no strain, no stress, no test, just to be swooped up into glory. Indeed:

O joy! O delight! should we go without dying,
No sickness, no sadness, no dread, and no crying,
Caught up through the clouds with our Lord into glory,
When Jesus receives His own.
(*It May be at Morn* SDA Hymnal # 207)

To fear death is to live in bondage. We could never live adventurously for God if we have not come to grips with the reality of our mortality. Indeed, as the paradox goes, 'Cowards die many times before their death'. Once is good enough. The truth makes you free... in more ways than one!

****

"When I Come to…. (Gulp) Die… Give Me Jesus."

——•◈•——

And I heard a voice from heaven saying unto me, Write, Blessed are the dead which die in the Lord from henceforth: Yea, saith the Spirit, that they may rest from their labours; and their works do follow them. Revelation 14:13

Precious in the sight of the LORD is the death of his saints. Psalm 116:15

Since we are on the issue of death, let me briefly recount a funny family incident. One morning, some years ago, at our morning family worship, we were singing the song *Give Me Jesus*. When we reached the part of the song which says 'Oh when I come to die…'my youngest daughter loudly declared: 'Stop, I do not like that song. Change it.' We all burst out laughing heartily. It was really funny how she did it. Yeah, we changed the song.

Dereka Lynn, much older now, is not alone in that feeling of aversion for death. While we may acknowledge being in bondage, as the Bible unarguably puts it, how can we unshackle ourselves? We really cannot. The chains are in the mind. God has to do it. Having a knowledge of theology will not do it either.

222

If God did not release me from that fearful bondage, I could never have traversed the valley in the way I have done. God replaces our fears with His peace. The Psalmist correctly states 'Though, I walk through the valley of the shadow of death I will fear no evil.' The enemies of faith are stymied when they see what is inexplicable to them.

I would strongly contend that the issue is not so much about when we die. Indeed, our times are in the hand of God. Additionally, I would be very cautious in giving anyone a time line, simply because ironically enough, my time, unknown to me, may very well come before the person I have placed on death row. There will always be life's little ironies!

It is unfortunate that we can become so bogged down with length of time that we forget that it is *quality of life* that God is looking for. One spiritual writer intimates that we have one lease on life and our main goals should be to discover how we can invest our powers that they yield the greatest profit, and how we can do the most for the glory of God, and the benefit of our fellowmen. Life is only valuable as it is used for these ends. (See Christian Temperance and Bible Hygiene, p 41)

In our brief stay on this earth, we have to be all about God and not all about self. Our purpose is not to impress others but to influence them for His Kingdom. Talk, though necessary, is cheap. Sacrificial living may be 'expensive' but its dividends are eternal!

****

Made To Be An Eagle

---•❋•---

But those who hope in the LORD will renew their strength. They will soar on wings like eagles; they will run and not grow weary, they will walk and not be faint. Isaiah 40:31 NIV

The person who is truly waiting on God, with their hopes placed solidly in Him, cannot then be sluggish, tired, miserable, complaining, scratching in the dust, eking out a meagre existence like a chicken, as opposed to soaring like the eagle. No! God never speaks false. If God makes a promise and our experience falls short of it, then let us not water down the Word of God or make it of no effect. The fault lies, *not with the Word*, but with us. In Psalm 89:34 God categorically states: I will not violate my covenant or alter what my lips have uttered. The power of the word is also represented in Isaiah 55:11: (NLT)

> *The rain and snow come down from the heavens and stay on the ground to water the earth. They cause the grain to grow, producing seed for the farmer and bread for the hungry. It is the same with my word. I send it out, and it always produces fruit. It will accomplish all I want it to, and it will prosper everywhere I send it.*

What powerful texts these all are! Has God sent His Word out into our lives and is it bearing fruit? I believe that the 'eagle life' is what God intended for us. We are designed to soar and do something with our lives to impact others for God. One spiritual writer makes the point that our entire lives are to be about God, furthering His plan and purpose, not simply living out our own agenda. God makes promises to enable us to carry out His divine purpose. His 'divine fiats' are not arbitrarily imposed on us. Our altitude in this life will depend on whether we believe God's promises, and we should, because He is really our biggest balcony fan!

Our Biggest Balcony Fan

But the tongue can no man tame; it is an unruly
evil, full of deadly poison. Therewith bless we
God, even the Father; and therewith curse
we men, which are made after the similitude
of God. Out of the same mouth proceedeth
blessing and cursing. My brethren, these
things ought not so to be. Doth a fountain
send forth at the same place sweet water and
bitter? James 3:8-11

The true Christian is a person who seeks to encourage others. The memorable concept of 'balcony and basement' people, I discovered in a book called *The Scent of Love* by Keith Miller. This concept purports that in your life there will be balcony and basement people. Balcony people are those who are rooting for you, they say things like: 'Great going. Keep it up! We know you can do it! We are praying for you.'

Such persons are positive and unselfishly speak blessings into your life. They wish you well. God has blessings in store for them. God told Abraham Genesis 1:3, "I will bless those who bless you, and whoever curses you, I will curse."

Basement people would be persons who use their tongues in negative and critical ways. Very sadly, not understanding their purpose in life, they spend time seeking to shoot down others. The book of Psalms outlines the behavior and activities of basement people. David in very graphic style, describes the behaviour of 'enemies' – his basement people.

Hide me from the secret plots of the wicked... who sharpen their tongue like a sword, and bend their bows to shoot their arrows - bitter words. Psalm 64:2 & 3 NKJV

Even Jesus had basement people, so as His followers we can expect no less. The Bible gives us excellent advice on how to handle them in Matthew 5:44-47.

However, we ourselves should aim to be balcony persons. We should even be balcony persons of those, who for whatever reason take umbrage against us. In my journey, God has blessed me with an entourage of wonderful balcony people. I have a prayer letter called "Input from Others" where those who have vicariously walked with me during this time, and have been reading the letters have documented their thoughts. My travellers strategically, and very wisely too, serve as witnesses.

****

The Essence of True Friendship

---●✦●---

*A friend is always loyal, and a brother is born
to help in time of need. Proverbs 17:7 NLT*

As I approach the end of my journey with you, I will now include
excerpts from the Prayer Letter collection called *Input From
Others*. It begins with an introductory comment, followed by
the thoughts of a long standing friend.

(This letter, Input from Others, was written more than five years
ago.) Dawn's comments were written eleven years ago.

*To My Readers: This journey could not have been the exciting, and
even enjoyable one it has been, if I did not have travellers. In a
sense they may have "climbed into my skin" and so they vicariously
walked with me. So far, they have not had to sing: "Abide with me;
fast falls the evening tide!"*

*Writing with a sense of a live audience inspired me to keep sharing
my goodies as they came in, as well as the not so goodies. It was
indeed therapeutic to be able to write, metaphorically speaking,
from the eye of the storm. My readers encouraged me, not only
with their presence, but by their responses to some of the letters.
Ingeniously, my travellers serve as witnesses, corroborating that
I wrote in the time frame outlined and that what I penned was a
bona fide account of my trek through the desert.*

We now hear from:

DAWN MINOTT (*SOUTH AFRICA*)

It was humbling to be considered a friend of Nola's and to be invited to accompany her on this journey that has been a life-changing experience for me. When I was struggling with understanding the "will of God" it was Nola who directed me to 'God's Waiting Room', and it is from that sacred place of waiting and watching for the manifestations of His will for my life that I have journeyed with her also watching for His manifestation in her life. This is a journey that has shown me what faith really is.

Nola's journey has also repositioned my understanding of faith. I've come to realize that her decision to submit her health completely to God's will is truly about expressing her faith and even more so, it's a powerful testimony about *Who she is expressing this faith in. Knowing full well that this journey may not only be through the shadow of death's valley but could lead to death, because she understands faith and because she knows that the God in whom her faith is anchored is able, she journeys continuously in His will. Having journeyed vicariously through the "valley" with her, I was encouraged to re-examine faith.*

I feel extremely privileged to have walked this valley with Nola, to be a part of what many would have deemed a private affair. Nola, you've used even your ill-health to strengthen me physically and spiritually, you could not have done a more selfless thing and I will be always grateful. You are my blessing and I thank and praise God for you. I love you around the world and back ~ Da

Comment: Dawn is one of my travellers who has stood unflinchingly by my side. I am impressed to include here, a poem which she composed, and gave to me in a lovely card in October 2003 when she was in Barbados. She also wrote another one of proleptic import. Dawn's poem inspired me to higher ground and I am challenged to be all that she lovingly envisions of me. Thanks Dawn! This is her composition:

Special Friend

One day God looked through the portals of time
And stopped at my page for a little while.
He saw days in my life when I wasn't as strong,
And everything I tried just turned out wrong.
And He thought, "What will I do to help my child?
Alas, I will give her a special friend", He decides.

He looked at you and your friendly way
Your laughter and spirit brightening a dark day,
A dedicated person, gracious and kind,
Always giving of yourself, never seeming to mind
Trustworthy and devoted, on you He can depend
So God gave you to me, to be my special friend.

Thank you for being a friend to me!
Dawn Minott
14 October 2003

End of the insert

January 2, 2013: A note about Dawn Minott.

Dawn left Barbados several years ago and currently resides in the United States. She is a compassionate Godly woman who knows how to mentor women. Dawn will be launching her new book in April. The title is: "Moments: A Heart Journey". It is of great significance that the title of her book reflects the kind of person that she is: one who can journey with you in her heart. The comments above, written over twelve years ago, are corroborative of her genuine nature. Dawn, your Barbadian family await their copy!

At this point in the further tweaking of the manuscript, Dawn resides in Nigeria.

****

Feasting On The Promises

———•◉•———

And the words of the Lord *are flawless, like silver purified in a crucible, like gold refined seven times. Psalm 12:6 NIV*

The final letter in my main publication is called *Passing The Baton of Faith* and here is an excerpt from that letter written May-July 2012:

What makes the huge difference in the outcome of our journey is whether we actually believe what God has said. The Word of God, words printed on a page, are essentially dead words, except they are believed. My strength in this long journey has been unabated because the Holy Spirit helped me to personally appropriate the promises found in the Bible for my special needs! The many verses of Scripture which I have tucked away in the depths of my heart have served to radiantly colour my mental landscape. I have never seen the sky as black and ominous. On the contrary, it has always shone brilliantly with the goodness of God.

As I have sat at the banquet table of God's Word, I have taken and devoured precious promises with great relish. What a feast I have had! I can identify with Jeremiah who said that he ate the word and it became the joy and rejoicing of his heart. (Jeremiah 15:16) God's Word has enabled me to retain a bouncing sense of humour throughout this journey. I smiled as I learnt that God does not delight in the strength of a horse, nor does he take pleasure in the legs of a man but "He takes pleasure in them that fear him, in them that hope in his mercy. Psalm 147:10 My hope has not been in vain! End of Excerpt

A NEW COMMENT

On Sabbath, August 24, 2013, I was invited to share with the Pinelands Church family at their 'Prayer and Fast' session. The topic I was given was *The Word of Truth.* What I shared there came out of my experience. It has come home to me very forcibly that the Word of God comes to us at the doctrinal level and it is very important to hold fast to correct doctrine.

However, there are two other levels to which my experiences have sensitized me. There are spiritual truths which are not doctrines 'per se'. For example, there are deep spiritual truths embedded in Job 22:28 and Mark 11:23. I will allow you to do your own foraging now. One may have a correct understanding of doctrine and yet be totally devastated by some unforeseen storm that bursts upon the life. Then the third level is that of personal truth. When God communicates a personal truth to you, in the context of your life's journey, then it becomes as powerful as the written Word and must be tenaciously held in the heart, no matter what! Read Romans 4: 17-21.

Of course, our human nature is so tricky and deceitful (see Jeremiah 17:9) and we can be more about our own agenda rather than the promotion of our Father's gracious character. So someone could claim that God gave him/her a directive, when in fact God did no such thing.

But, as I often like to say, 'Time is its own expositor'. It is therefore excellent divine strategy to have two most important caveats to keep us all in line: the will of God and the honour of His name.

Those boundaries, firmly established, allow us to claim the wonderful promises of God's Word, spoken to us individually, or extracted from the written Word.

The following quotation is indeed very timely:

> The Scriptures are to be received as God's Word to us, not written merely, but spoken... when *He said to the woman of Capernaum, "Daughter, be of good comfort: thy faith hath made thee whole; go in peace," He spoke to other afflicted, sin-burdened ones who should seek His help.....So with all the promises of God's Word. In them He is speaking to us individually, speaking as directly as if we could listen to His voice. It is in these promises that Christ communicates to us His grace and power.*[53]

The formula seems quite simple to me. Try it!

****

[53] Ellen G. White, *The Faith I Live By*, Review and Herald Publishing Association, Washington, D.C (1958) p 9

The Power of What You *Say*

---•❈•---

*For verily I say unto you, That whosoever shall
say unto this mountain, Be thou removed, and
be thou cast into the sea; and shall not doubt
in his heart, but shall believe that those things
which he saith shall come to pass; he shall
have whatsoever he saith. Mark 11:23*

I am told that you can never rise above your confession. In
the walk of faith, the power of words and their effect are often
minimized, if not totally misunderstood.

Though some have claimed "ill health" for me, innocently so, and
not with any unkind intention, I have never claimed it for myself.
Why? Did God not tell me in my heart that I would walk through
the valley of the shadow of death, standing up? Am I not aware
of changes which have occurred in my body? Am I trying to be
an ostrich? Well, the legs might easily qualify me, but not the
head in the sand! A BMI which is out of range, obviously not on
the overweight side, speaks its tale.... but not a tale of woe, as I
look through God's Divine lens.

In their book *The Power of Your Words*, the writers Don Gossett
and E.W. Kenyon share some explosive and even debatable
principles.

They clearly intimate that if your testimony is one of sickness, then that will develop the sickness stronger in your body. In the face of sickness, they advocate that you should courageously let your testimony be that of God's own Word. I contend that as long as an individual brings bona fide faith and prayer into a situation, that person *simply cannot relate to circumstances in the same way as another individual who has not done that.*

The writers postulate that when we depart from the Word of God to feelings or appearances, that is how we will be defeated. We need to understand that the greatest victory we can win as Christians is when everything cries out 'Impossible!' They further maintain that it can be our experience when we dare to hold fast our confession of God's Word, that impossibilities can become realities.

Ignorance of the spiritual law that when you state a thing, you actually decree it into your life will work against those who constantly think and speak negatively. I guess we could call it the 'law of the mouth'. People may speculatively 'decree' for us, but that is of no consequence because the Word says that *no weapon* that is formed against the Christian can prosper. What is critical is *what we decree for ourselves!*

So you may justifiably ask: 'Is this not some kind of psychological gimmick? Some slick, sleazy, sly, mentally manipulative trick?' In the secular realm, it may manifest itself in that way. If someone is trying to palm off some product on an unsuspecting person, of course he will speak very positively and make great claims for his product.

However, in the spiritual realm, speaking positively about unseen realities (a neat paradox) is a bona fide principle, properly applied within the boundaries of the will of God and bringing honour to His name.

The above caveats (God's will and honour) will prevent the presumptuous, fanatical and self-willed individuals from successfully claiming from the sublime to the ridiculous under the guise of that *"whatsoever"* of Mark 11:33.

Forms of the verb 'to say' are used in the text three times. We must *speak* our belief and our belief must be rooted *in the Word of God.*

The virulent and vehement, overt *and covert*, critics of faith do not understand the power of the Word, the power of positive speech and the power of a positive confession!!

The writers declare: "Some folk are always confessing their faith in diseases, their faith in failure and calamity. You will hear them confessing that their children are disobedient, and that their husband or wife is not doing what is right. They constantly confess failure and doubts. *They little realise that that confession robs them of their ability and efficiency."* (My italics)[54]

I am sure this will raise some questions which could lead to a good spirited discussion. However, for those who do not understand the power of confession i.e. what comes out of your mouth, take note:

> "Your confession is the expression of your faith, and these confessions of lack and of sickness shut out the Father God out of your life and let Satan in, giving him the right-of-way. Confession of failure, give disease and failure dominion over your life. They honour Satan and rob God of His glory."[55]

---

[54] Donn Gossett and E. W. Kenyon, *The Power of Your Words* (Kenyon Gospel Publishing Society, Inc, P.O Box 973, Lynnwood, Washington, 98036), pg. 109

[55] Ibid, pg. 109

As we say, the proof of the pudding is always in the eating, so we will only know if all of this is mere rhetoric or there is truth in it. The Word says that time and chance happens to every man. When your time and chance come, I encourage you to be a faith man or a faith woman and confess that:

You are not lacking any good thing because 'no good thing will God withhold from them that walk uprightly'. Psalm 84:11.

Confess that God has not 'given you a spirit of fear but of power and of love and of a sound mind'. 2 Tim 1:7

Confess that you are not weak for 'the Lord will give strength unto his people'. Psalm 29:11.

And of course, where applicable, confess in clarion tones: 'I shall not die but live, and shall declare the works *and* recount the illustrious acts of the Lord'. Psalm 118:17. (Amplified Bible)

Need we confess more?

In Honour To God

·•❁•·

I am the LORD; that is my name. I will not give my glory to anyone else or the praise I deserve to idols. Isaiah 42:8 (God's Word Translation)

My duty, but more my desire to God, my Dad, my Friend Jesus, and my travelling Companion, the Holy Spirit is to glorify Their name in every respect. As a line from the song *To God Be The Glory*, says: "... and should I gain any praise let it go to Calvary..."

I can say that the kudos for all of what God has empowered me to do must go to Calvary. The fact that I am standing here, some eleven years after I commenced my faith and health adventure with God is stupendous credit to the mercy and faithfulness of God. If there is anything positive to be said about my life on this earth, then it certainly must all go to Calvary.

Even though, I am out of range for my BMI, obviously not on the overweight end, the fact is, I am still standing. I have stood in all of the strength that God has copiously poured into me. Recently, I listened to a video where it was said that someone responded to a question about his wellbeing by saying: "I am vertical and ventilating." A cute and humorous response, but 'vertical and ventilating' is just the very basic. I am doing more than that. I am enjoying abundant life in Christ and not only is my cup overflowing, but so is my belly. The Word says: 'He that believeth on me, as the scripture hath said out of his belly shall flow rivers of living waters.' (John 7:38 KJV)

What has been shared in this publication is but a trickle of water in comparison with what is to come. Both works are designed as documented memorials to the honour and glory of God. Documenting our bona fide experiences with God is very important and is supported by Biblical counsel. God told Moses in Exodus 17:14: 'Write this on a scroll as something to be remembered and make sure that Joshua hears it.' Also in Exodus 24:27 we have recorded:

Then the Lord said to Moses, 'Write down these words, for in accordance with these I have made a covenant with you and with Israel.'

Of course, one of the big advantages in documenting and publishing is that long after you are gone, your works will still be speaking. I am exceptionally thrilled that starting in 2003, I obeyed the promptings of the world's wisest Counsellor, who well knows that the pen is mightier than the sword. Even when our journey is completed and we are laid to rest and can no longer praise God, ((Psalms 115:17, 18 KJV) our works can still have an even more powerful impact. In reading a person's work, you will unwittingly find yourself assessing that individual and determining whether his/her testimony is genuine or spurious. Better yet, if you actually knew the individual and found no discrepancy between what he/she said and what was lived.

The first yet unpublished manuscript which comprises the Prayer Letters contains one letter which I wrote to God. Most Christians believe in the Trinity. There is one God, but three distinct beings who perform different roles. I wrote a letter of thanks to each One of them. I will share the one I wrote to my Heavenly Dad:

PRAYER LETTER TO THE TRIUNE GOD April 2009 (This one is to my "Daddy God.")

Dear God, It is fitting that the final letter should be written to You. Though You are One God, yet You manifest Yourself in three distinct personalities. I accept this by faith and my valley experience has certainly corroborated that unalterable truth. All three of You have functioned in different ways in my experience.

My Heavenly Dad, let me start with You. You have been truly like a father to me in every sense of the word. You, of all Persons, know how very much that means to me. No matter how old I may become, I will always think of myself as being your little girl – the little girl whose Dad told her to jump ....and she did. You caught me, as expected and carried me, as only a true Father could.

Sometimes I ponder my birth. My young inexperienced Mum held me (still her one and only child) up to Heaven and asked You to bless me. You heard that prayer. You have cared for and sustained me all the days of my life. Particularly, through the experience of the last five years have You led me, and washed me in incredible blessings! I have never lacked for Your care, love, support and comfort. There has never been a question in my mind that I am your daughter ....born twice!

You have told me in your Word that your Spirit would witness with my spirit that I am a child of God. I am humbled to think of myself as a daughter of God. I do not take that privilege lightly at all. And Dad, I accept the responsibilities which come with it. I must never sully the 'Family Name'.

Dad, I am 'blown away' by the fact that even before I was born, You had written every day of my existence in my book of life. What a thought! Though my birth may have appeared to have been a 'mistake', yet You had an awesome plan for my life. From the outset of my valley walk, I had the deeply implanted assurance that You would be with me and that You had already given the nod, so to speak, that it was done, while it was being done!

My Dad, I am very happy that the fear I had of you as a teenager is no longer there. I must admit that in the Old Testament You do seem somewhat austere. But as I have grown with You over the years, I have come to view You very differently. You are the same God in the Old Testament as You are in the New. Nothing split about Your personality. I love the poem You inspired me to compose, 'In God's Darkroom'. I have seen You with the eyes of my heart, and Your face, with kind and tender eyes, is indelibly imprinted on my soul.

Thank you very much for carrying me right through this experience, as You promised to do. You reminded me of the immutability of Your Word. You do not lie. You will never renege on Your promise to Your child. You have been so faithful! I must say Dad, the assurances in Your Word are second to none! As you know, my biggest concern was that I did not disappoint You. I did not want to bring disgrace on Your Name – to be a black sheep of the family. You provided for my needs so extravagantly that I was reduced to tears many times. You were really my Father who mothered me. I experienced your love as a mother's love and also as a husband's love. As a mother would, You tenderly nurtured me and were very attentive to all my needs. As my divine Husband, I could feel your passionate love for me!

Very real in my soul was the strong, kind, deep reassurance that I was very special to you and that the crucible did not mean disfavour, but quite the opposite. You told me in Your word that You would quiet me with Your love. That love, a romantic kind of love, was not one which whispered 'sweet nothings' but 'awesome somethings'. You quietly inscribed messages deep in my heart which stabilized me and strengthened to such an extent that the enemies which would have wanted to attack and weaken my spiritual defences were bound and gagged.

Thank you Dad for enabling me to see that Your will is always the very best thing! Thank you too for reminding me in Your word that if our earthly parents, though fallible, can give good gifts to us as their children, what about You, as our Heavenly Parent. Your gifts may not all be wrapped in 'pretty Christmas paper" but certainly they are the ones that will bring us the greatest good and will enable us to live the purpose for which we were created.

Dad, when I think about it, this experience has been a 'lay floating' experience with You.

You have been like a big bed of water under me. I have been able to relax, very comfortably, no panic lurking in the shadows, never doubting that You could bear my weight, not that it is a lot now! Thankfully, I did not consider how far away the ocean bed was, that was not to be my concern. Having completely abandoned myself to Your care, I have no regrets at all! This has been, and is being such a deep experience. Well, You sure took me out into the deep, not to drown me but to teach me the skill of laying floating on You. But I also realize that some lessons cannot be taught on the safety of the shore. You have to take us into 'dangerous waters'.

Finally Dad, thank You for placing Your love in my heart as You promised You would do. You have not failed me in any respect. None whatsoever! I am supremely happy in the way You have handled my case, the gentle manner in which You have dealt with me. I am glad that I do not have to fake any emotion with You. There is nothing fake about You, either my Dad. You are exactly what You claim to be.

You assured me in my heart that it makes You very happy when I place a high demand on You. You can see in my innermost soul, which no one else can do. You see the depth to which I have cast my entire being on You, confident that You are a God of Your word. I am thrilled to have a Father like you. I feel honoured and deeply humbled that You could actually call me, a sinner saved by grace, Your Daughter! I dare not look a gift horse in the mouth. As I continue my life's journey, I know that Your goodness and mercy will follow me all the days of my life ....to the very last day on this earth!

On Your Mark! Get Set! Go!

————————•❁•————————

Therefore, since we are surrounded by such a great cloud of witnesses, let us throw off everything that hinders and the sin that so easily entangles. And let us run with perseverance the race marked out for us, fixing our eyes on Jesus, the pioneer and perfecter of faith. Hebrews 12: 1&2 NIV

Finally, we have come to the end. I truly enjoyed sharing with you and engaging your interest for a little while. I trust that your appetite has been whetted for the full publication and that you were blessed and inspired. Though we are at the end of our writing/reading journey, the race of our individual lives continues.

Life is often 'metaphorised' not only as a journey, but also as a race. In our spiritual race, Jesus is the starter and finisher of our life of faith. We are running this race to please Him and to bring honour to His name. I cannot help but recollect that outstanding run by Superman Felix Sanchez in the London 2012 Olympics. Unforgettable indeed!

I was most intrigued when I saw him drop to the ground at the end of the race. Taking a photograph from beneath his identification number, he kissed it reverently. I immediately surmised that it must have been a picture of someone whom he loved dearly and that person had probably died, so the race was for that 'someone'.

My curiosity was even more piqued at the medal ceremony where he wept uncontrollably. I knew his weeping had to be connected to the action of kissing the photograph. It was a very moving scene. I must admit that, 'lachrymosal creature' as I am, I cried to see such an unabashed display of emotion. I knew it had to be more than the usual 'medal emotion'. I did some research on the Internet and my surmising was indeed confirmed.

Winning that race was for his beloved 'abuela'. His grandmother had passed away on August 16, 2008, the very day he was involved in eliminations in Beijing. He was so grief stricken that he competed without will and was eliminated. Sanchez is reported to have said: "The day she died in Beijing it broke my heart. That's why I ran with the picture close to my heart." He also said: "I made a promise that day that I would win a medal for her... it took me four years."

As I pondered the details of Sanchez's saga, I could not help but make a major personal spiritual leap of application. Like Sanchez, I am also running a race, not for my abuela, but for my Best Friend Jesus, who ran a race for me when He became a human being. I am not running this race to bring glory to myself, but a well-run race will bring glory to my Best Friend.

We extol and give much honour and many accolades to human beings. What about God? Don't we sometimes, many times, accord far more honour, praise and adulation to mere mortals than we do to our God, who subjected Himself to a very shameful and ignominious death for each of us?

Understanding this at a deep personal level should result in our seeing that our entire lives must be an investment for God. We must give our all in the spiritual realm to running a race which will bring to our God, all the honour and glory, which He so richly deserves. There is no trial run; we only have one chance in the race of life.

The memory of Sanchez's illustrious run will fade with the passing of time and he will be forgotten. The true purpose for our existence lies beyond our achievements in this life, honourable and laudable as they may be. We need a deeper consciousness that the reason for our existence is to glorify God, which in essence, is a showcasing of His loving and compassionate character.

To successfully run our race, we cannot afford to have any weights which would impede our progress. Unbelief is a weight, a millstone around our necks which will surely bring us down, drowning us in a sea of doubt, dismay and discouragement. However, faith in God and the promises of His word frees us to be all that God intended us to be when He first thought of us. Faith frees us to run our race with passion, grace, determination, discipline and dedication. It's not an easy race because the prize we are running to attain cost our Lord His very life. So, it's not a cheap race. It must cost us something.

We are not running this race for Olympic gold which will perish, but for an inheritance which is reserved in Heaven for us. (1Peter 1:4) And, as we run we are kept by the power of God. Sanchez, apparently had the word 'abuela' stitched into his spikes. It was all about his beloved grandmother. Quite touching actually!

For me, it must be all about Jesus. That name far more powerful than any other name in all the universe must be stitched in my running shoes. That name must be close to my heart. I can never successfully run my race without a robust faith and confidence in God.

He is the one who will say, 'Well done'. Like the Apostle Paul, we must be able to say with confidence, "I have fought a good fight, I have finished my course, I have kept the faith." (2 Timothy 4:7)

So, may I pass the baton of faith to you? No one can run your leg of the race. We have come too far by faith to turn back now. Good! You have grabbed the baton! Now run... and don't you stop until you breast that tape!!!

Epilogue

---············❋············---

"There is a tide in the affairs of men which, taken at the flood, leads on to fortune; omitted, all the voyage of their life is bound in shallows and in miseries. On such a full sea are we now afloat, and we must take the current when it serves or lose our ventures."
(Julius Caesar Act IV Scene 2, Lines 269–276)

Brutus, the speaker, is figuratively referring to a "tide" in the lives of human beings: if an individual takes advantage of the high tide, he may float out to sea and travel far; however, if he misses this chance, the "voyage" that his life comprises will remain forever confined to the shallows, and he will never experience more than the mundane events in the narrow little bay in which he finds himself. So such an individual, male or female, must "take the current" and not miss out on opportunities.

When we transfer that bit of Shakespearean erudition into the spiritual realm, what tremendous life lessons and principles we discover. Life is metaphorised, using different images and certainly the sea voyage metaphor is quite applicable. If I consider my life to be a sea voyage, then I would have to say that I am glad that I was able to 'take the current'. In a literal sense, taking the current represents my decision in 2003 to follow God's directive with respect to the recommended procedure, as previously outlined in the recounting of the saga.

There is always a supernatural working in the affairs of men, not recognised by some, and therefore such persons will not only miss their opportunities to go with the flow of God's tide, but will be critical of others who choose to do so.

This notion of 'a tide in the affairs of men' may be kept confined to the literary arena, but transferred to the spiritual realm, we can apply it to our own lives and learn some important life lessons. God's overarching strategic plan is all about our eternal salvation and that of others. That awareness was dropped in my spirit at the outset of my journey. As I continue to go with the flow of God's current and not try to swim *against* it, I will in essence be living my life's purpose, accomplishing my divine mission.

I again make reference to one of my favourite books, 'God Sent a Man' where the writer postulates that there is a definite life plan shaped for each of us and it is the glory of our lives to do the thing which God has marked for us to do. (See page 53, God sent a Man)

I believe that truth one hundred percent and this belief has coloured and shaped my journey. I unreservedly concur with the writer when he intimates that if we *really* accept that truth and live it:

> *"...There can never be any place in our lives for despondency, for discouragement. We live in God's thought and all that enters our lives is for a purpose; and that purpose is a plan of God. How it glorifies all life just to believe that. Our lives will glow with beauty, strength, meaning, and enthusiasm as we make this great truth our own, and learn to abide in God's will."*[56]

---

[56] Carlyle B. Haynes, God Sent A Man, Review and Herald Publishing Association, Washington, DC 20039 (1962) p 52

That is a very powerful statement indeed!!

I agree with Carlyle B. Haynes' spiritual insight, not simply as a truth to hold in my head, but more so as truth to energise my heart. In the crucible of my life, it has been tested and it has stood the test of time, literally and figuratively! My voyage, or health adventure with God, commenced in 2003 when I was 46 old. In September 2013 I turned 57. I have had many years to test the validity of the deep spiritual truth Haynes has offered to us.

In a sense, my journey has been soft and gentle, but not without its obstacles to overcome. One has been the battle with self and overcoming a perverted appetite. It has not been a walk over! Not at all! However, the Best Lover of my soul has offered me His shoulder, not to cry on, but to stand on, so that I could stretch, *and be stretched,* to reach my full potential in Him. Yes, we could label it a 'hot stretch' to utilise some jargon from my gym. My walk has been *fully persuasive* of the reality that God *never* forsakes His own... *never!* His perfect strength is available right to the very end of our lives. **(See Job 5:26 NIV)**

It has been a full ten years of walking by faith... and not by sight; a journey where I have been gratefully imbibing some wonderful and very deep spiritual lessons. In His awesome planning for us, at the individual level, God at times has to shut us away to teach us. I deeply appreciate the spiritual insight which this writer draws from a story in 2 Kings Chapter 4. Verse 4 reads: Thou shalt shut the door upon thyself and upon thy sons. The writer essays that at times:

> "...God will form a mysterious wall around us, and cut away all props, and all the ordinary ways of doing things and shut us up to something divine

which is utterly new and unexpected, something
that old circumstances do not fit into...[57]

This comment epitomises my journey. I may not be able to predict the details of my unfolding journey, but yet I know, with certainty, that God is working out everything for my best good. In essence, I am obeying the Biblical injunction to walk by faith and not by sight. Then again, we need not be blind to the stupendous promises of God and the character of the One who has made them.

Additionally, that mysterious wall which has shut me in with God, has also mercifully served to shut out the enemies of faith, so that I have not been discouraged. The deep truth of the matter is that if you want to do more than simply attend church and warm the bench, you must be prepared to embark on a journey with God. Some people want a marvellous testimony, but they want it at a very cheap cost. They desire a testimony without any test.

I would rather walk the high adventurous road with God than subsist in a treadmill existence. The writer further intimates that most religious people tend to live mundane and rather predictable lives. However, the persons which He leads out, in a sense, on special adventures:... "He shuts in where all they know is that God has hold of them and their expectation is from Him alone." [58]

Walking with God in a faith journey could never be boring and it will be the most teachable moment of your life. Sometimes, I feel as if I am in the 'Harvard of Heaven' being tutored by the world's Best Teacher. He has shown me, as we have travelled together over the years, some awesome spiritual truths directly

---

[57] Streams in the Desert, April 5
[58] Ibid

from His Word, and also through various deep spiritual writers. The book *Streams in the Desert*, is a must read, if you want to go deeper with God.

Our journeying with God, *and to God*, in our brief life span can also be conceptualized under the metaphor of our being clay, and God being the Potter. Other spiritual truths can be learnt through the symbolism of the potter and the clay. God had to reshape me in more ways than one.

Becoming that malleable clay, with which God could work, has facilitated my being shaped for His purpose. Had I been stiff and resistant, what stress and unnecessary pain I would have caused myself. It has been a very exciting experience, to say the least, to have fitted in with God's plan for my life, rather than trying to dictate to Him. There can be no turning back now.

Over the years, as I have shared with various church congregations and groups, I have prefaced my talks by saying that God had to remove two fears from me to enable me to share with ease and utmost positivity - the fear of death and the fear of people. Both of these fears can so cripple an individual that he may be unable to 'step out of the box', and into God's plan for his life. One spiritual writer postulates that God has a way of seeming to work against Himself but His plans for His trusting children are not just excellent ... they are par excellent!

Of special import, and application, is the following spiritual insight:

> *"We may not see now the outcome of the beautiful plan which God is hiding in the shadow of His hand; it yet may be long concealed; but faith may be sure that He is sitting on the throne, calmly waiting*

the hour when, with adoring rapture, we shall say,
"All things have worked together for good." [59]

I have travelled the last ten years, not without sorrow. I witnessed over forty persons complete their life's journey... all coming out of a health situation. Some were friends, others were family. Notably, quite a few of those individuals I encountered, I did not know before. I only met them when it was strategic for me to do so. *'Faith in the furnace ... and no heat!'* documents several of those encounters, some of which are memorably touching.

My strategic connection to some individuals actually started in 2002. In her valley time, God impressed me to share words of comfort and assurance with a lady. That episode of our brief moments together was documented in our local newspaper, The Nation, in an article entitled: 'Divine Inspiration'. I did not give the article its title. (See Appendix)

It is my hope that your appetite has indeed been whetted for that second completed, but yet unpublished work. Some of my canny adventures, as the protagonist of the drama, are fully outlined there. If God had not poured His incredible and inexhaustible strength into me, I could not possibly have accomplished the feat of writing two books while walking through the valley of the shadow of death. I always tell God that I owe Him my life, for the rest of my life!!

Initially, I was all about a 'quick fix'. Most, if not all of us, are wired that way. "Lord, get me out of this, and get me out fast!" Had God followed my time frame, or answered my prayers according to my myopic vision, obviously neither of the two publications would have come to fruition. What would I have written about? The journey provided the material. I did not have to concoct stuff. The journey is indeed *stranger than fiction.*

---

[59] Streams in the Desert, August 30

I believe that God's long range strategic plan for my life included my writing. Before I was born, it was written in my Book of Life that I would write at least two books. There may be more, who knows? Thankfully, I submitted to God's impeccable timing and the blessings are still being poured out. I was well tutored to understand many deep spiritual lessons and these I have sought to teach my own children.

God has a plan for each of us, written before we were even born. We do not need to concoct a plan and give it to Him. Simply find out what *His plan is and work with that plan*. It will indeed be the winning plan. One spiritual writer advocates excellent advice:

> *Let God form your plans about everything in your mind and heart and then let Him execute them. Do not possess any wisdom of your own.* [60]

He further cautions that in the execution of God's plan it may well *seem a*s if God is working against Himself but our task is simply to listen, obey and trust that God knows exactly what He is doing, even if it appears otherwise. It is a nice paradox to say that those who walk by faith have a much clearer vision than those who walk by sight!

The endorsers of that yet unpublished work, Dr. Andrew Harewood, Pastor James Daniel, Pastor John Josiah and Mr. Robert Bobby Morris (now Barbados' Ambassador to the CARICOM), attest by their comments, that "Faith in the Furnace..... and no heat!" is a must read.

Until we meet again, I trust that reading "The Big Secret ..." has been a real blessing to you and that you caught the intended irony in the title.

---

[60] Streams in the Desert October 3

All kudos to our wonderful Dream Team: God our wonderful and compassionate Father, Jesus, our High Priest, rooting for us in the Holy of Holies and our very special "in House Friend", the Holy Spirit.

With such a team, it can be nothing less than ... 'Mission... POSSIBLE!'

October 12, 2013

Resistance Training at the Gym

Working Out at Home

Home Grown Sprouts- Part of a Healthy Lifestyle

Posing ...For Now.

Various Health Products Used

Work Horse Champion Juicer and Natural Foods

Home Workout Session. Lunges with Weights

Relaxing Amidst Beautiful Caribbean Scenery

Appendix 1

————————•◉•————————

This article is reprinted with the kind permission of the Nation Publishing Co. Limited.

The following article was featured in the December 2011 edition of The Nation Newspaper's BETTER HEALTH MAGAZINE in the column *'Hell Being 2 Well Being'*. I was interviewed by one of their reporters who then wrote up the article. We did have a bit of back and forth before we arrived at what was finally published. I express special appreciation to Kathy-Ann Best and Tracy Moore for their part in facilitating the publication of the article.

FIGHTING FIBROIDS WITH FAITH

Contributor: Kathy Ann Best

Photograph: Amery Butcher

Faith in God is in an intrinsic part of divine healing. Nola Estwick embarked on a journey of faith and progressive healing that would radically change her life.

In April 2003 Nola realized that she was steadily losing weight even though she had not changed her diet or lifestyle in any way. Normally weighing between 120 and 130 pounds, Nola went down to approximately 118 pounds and her tummy was distended.

Though she had no pain or other symptoms of illness, this constant weight loss troubled her. On visiting the doctor, he determined that she had fibroids and a hysterectomy was recommended. As a mother of grown children, Nola saw no reason not to have the procedure done.

Prior to the scheduled operation in July 2003, a friend she had not seen in more than 20 years told her that God would like to heal her and give her a powerful testimony.

"This statement caused me to realize that I had a choice. Not to choose is to choose. I didn't have to have the surgery. I expected then that God would guide me in the way I should go," Nola said.

Previously she had simply accepted unquestioningly what the doctor said, which seemed quite logical and sensible.

"I was not having any more children, so why keep a troublesome uterus?" Nola thought.

As a devout Christian, Nola immediately prayed about the situation, seeking God's input on the matter. After her prayer, she was led to a book called **Streams In The Desert** that gave her divine assurance about her decision.

As time progressed, she continued to lose weight and received the impression that God would let her go through the valley of the shadow of death standing up.

The first thing Nola did was to have an anointing service at her home. She knew that miracles could happen and expected God to miraculously "quick fix" her ailment, but this was not to be.

Nola recalled getting up one night around 2 a.m. in early December 2003 to go to the washroom: "After using the bathroom, I was thinking that I would do some reading when I noticed a figure crouched on the stairs.

"In amazement, I looked at the strange man hiding in my home. Realizing that he had been seen, the stranger stood up and started up the stairs towards me," she noted.

He quietly passed directly in front of her with his head bowed and went into nearby bedroom where he escaped through a window.

With her husband out of the island at the time, she screamed, awakening the rest of the household. The police were contacted but by the time they had arrived, the intruder was long gone, leaving only his footprints.

This episode, however, left a deep impression on Nola's mind.

To her, it meant God had revealed to her, that in the same way He protected her from the intruder, He would protect her from this ailment.

That same month, Nola went to see a homeopathic practitioner.

Though she was a vegetarian, Nola realized that she was not eating enough vegetables or drinking enough water.

"The visit was revealing. I have been a lacto-ovo-vegetarian for many years and was surprised to learn that my nutrition was very poor. The first thing I was told was that I was losing muscle and that the uterus was a symptom and not the cause of my trouble," she explained.

If confirmation was needed that she had made the right decision, this was it. Nola was placed on a program that involved exercise and an improved eating plan.

"First, I did a detox program and lost even more weight," she added. Nola was now down to 109 pounds. This, of course, caused many people to cast doubt on her decision for spiritual healing but Nola was determined to do things God's way.

"I knew that radical faith would have to be an intrinsic part of the journey. Faith that God was guiding correctly, that the remedial agencies of nature could effect progressive healing over time, and that the body has a built-in healing mechanism which can be used to our advantage," she told BETTER HEALTH.

She joined a gym and started doing resistance exercises. On her first visit to the gym, she did a range of exercises involving muscles that had lain dormant and were well-nigh seized up.

"At the end of the hour-long session, the trainer looked at me gleefully and said: 'Ya feel good, nuh?' I looked at him weakly and wondered if there was some measure of sadism to the comment. Nola recalled dragging herself to the car.

"I slumped into the seat, put my head on the steering wheel and wept. I felt absolutely awful. My stomach wanted to revolt. I wondered if I even had the strength to drive home. I thought I would have had to call the others at home to come and rescue me, but I made it home," she said.

She remembered that this bad feeling persisted until midday. For a while, going to the gym was a struggle as she was very weak, but she was able to increase her weight and can now leg-press up to 200 pounds.

She also learnt how to do sprouting, which is the practice of germinating seeds to be eaten either raw or cooked. They are a convenient way to have fresh vegetables for salads, and can be germinated at home or produced industrially.

Sprouts are believed to be highly nutritious and rich in enzymes that promote good health. They are the prominent ingredient of the raw food diet.

She also began juicing vegetables daily. She learnt the importance of using raw food, like uncooked vegetables, and gradually she started to regain weight but it fluctuated.

Through this lifestyle change, Nola learnt the importance of nutrition: "You need to feed your cells and not merely to satisfy your stomach.

"I saw that when the laws of health are violated, nature utters her protest. I was not eating properly or getting enough rest," she admitted.

Lack of rest, she learnt, contributes to the body becoming acidic-which she was told was one of her problems.

Nola learnt the important lesson of taking responsibility for compromising her health. Having surgery would have taken away all the essential life–changing truths that Nola learnt.

"Healing is much more than God giving you a miracle," Nola said, "it is about teaching you and showing you why your health was compromised in the first place."

Her tummy was deflated down to a normal size. She has a lot more energy. She is fitter than she has ever been.

People are often amazed at how strong she is, though still not at her regular weight. "I love going to the gym now and though the weights I use are nothing compared to the other guys, it's quite good compared to the ladies there," she said spiritedly.

It has been eight years since Nola's first visit to the homeopathic practitioner, and she is convinced that the natural path was the best way to go.

However, she insisted that her shared experiences were not meant to be prescriptive - she is not telling anyone what to do or not do in a similar situation.

Over the years she had a variety of tests done for malignancy. None of them to date have been conclusive. She spoke of a non-specific test (called the ESR) done in 2003, which she had to repeat in subsequent years. In 2004 it was 109, and it gradually decreased to 20 when done later. The doctor told Nola, that the highest this ESR should read is 15.

People will talk and may still think Nola is crazy for refusing surgery but that decision changed her diet and lifestyle and has left her more radiant and healthier. The complete trust she placed in God has caused her to feel more joy, exuberance, and energy. She is filled with more praise.

Nola opined, "I know that we should never be dismayed by gossips. Protection is provided in the word of God. I know that my healing is as a result of my faith.

"I now can better care for myself and my family and never lose an opportunity to help others. The impact on my family has been tremendous; they have all started to eat much better, using a lot more vegetables and fruits.

During this entire process I have only lost three weeks of teaching time as it relates to my health, which was during exam time in 2004 but while I was at home I was able to correct all my exam papers and add my marks.

"From that time until now I have stood before my students as an English Literature teacher discussing themes of death, courage and resilience," Nola said.

Due to her 31-year relationship with God, Nola sought guidance. Her faith in God involved accepting what He said and walking in that confidence no matter what.

Nola told BETTERHEALTH that she continues to do well.

"But my stance has always been, and will always be, that whatever say future tests say or do not say, I am standing my ground in the strength of God in the natural pathway," Nola commented.

"Real unswerving trust in God is imperative," Nola explained.

"What you say with your mouth should line up with what God has said. Many folks allow circumstances to overwhelm them, but genuine faith rises above circumstances."

Appendix 2

———————— ·❁· ————————

This article is reprinted with the kind permission of the Nation Publishing Co. Limited. It was published in The Nation Newspaper September 26, 2011 in the Herbs and Healing column by Annette Maynard Watson - teacher and herbal educator.

BELIEVING IN WORDS OF PROMISE

"You cannot claim the promises of divine healing while flagrantly breaking the laws of health and the laws of your being."

Words spoken by Mrs. Nola Estwick, a dedicated Christian and a Senior Teacher at the Christ Church Foundation School.

Estwick's health journey commenced in 2003. It was a very rich and rewarding experience. September 2010 climaxed seven years of continuous writing.

Estwick describes her amazing adventure as stemming from a choice, which was actually a leap in faith. It led her to assert: "With God all things are possible."

True Faith

Often confused with its wily impostor – presumption- genuine faith radically obeys God and stands on His word, regardless of the outcome. It is a critical component of divine healing.

Estwick explained that in July, 2003, as a result of unexplained weight loss, a hysterectomy because of fibroids was recommended.

In December 2003, a visit to a naturopathic practitioner indicated that the root of the problem needed to be addressed.

She inferred it was a grave situation. Since she could see her ribs clearly without an X-ray machine, Estwick knew this was the real McCoy. Not deviating from normal practice, she prayed about the matter. God then revealed to her that she would go through the Valley of the Shadow of Death standing up and impressed her to document the journey. She never had that surgery.

Estwick travelled peacefully and garnered confidence in the valley by resting on the promises of God, namely, Psalm 118:17 and Jeremiah 17: 7 & 8. They represented her Rhema word.

Additionally, there was a very uncanny encounter with a 'midnight intruder' which God providentially used to foreshadow her journey.

Uncertain of the route God would take, Estwick naively thought that God would 'quick fix' her. A 'quick fix' would have meant missing her two celebratory 'shout of faith' thanksgiving services. She would also have missed meeting the many wonderful persons across Barbados with whom she shared her aspects of her adventure.

Having sensibly torn up her itinerary to follow God's, she cannot wait to publish her amazing adventures. Estwick's progressive healing involved eating living foods. However, she insists that an entire lifestyle change involves the synergistic approach of doing a number of things, which will work in sync with the body's natural healing mechanism.

She also noted that the will to live or die is also in the mind. What people say about you or to you cannot hurt you, except you allow it to. Positive inner self-talk is tremendously therapeutic!

In conclusion, Estwick reinforced that her most significant learning experience was fully understanding that God is "a Man of His Word".

Estwick noted: "If God says it is done, well then, it dun! We can put our neck on the very block of His Word . . . and live!

Appendix 3

---·•❀•·---

This article is reprinted with the kind permission of the Nation Publishing Co. Limited. It was originally printed in the Nation Newspaper on June 18, 2012 and the contributor is Annette Maynard-Watson

HEALING HERBS: Positive Thoughts Way to Health

(Annette Maynard-Watson)

June 18, 2012

Father's Day was a grand celebration for men in Barbados. Many took the time to reflect on themselves and their families. I hope they also reflected on the silent doctors.

In this thought-provoking interview with Nola Estwick, a colleague on the health team, she offers these words of inspiration: "Positive healing thoughts can be categorized as silent doctors. The power and control the mind has over the body is generally underestimated.

"Research shows that chemical reactions are produced throughout the body by our thoughts, emotions and interactions with others.

"This awareness means that there is really no such thing as 'just a thought'. What is known as the 'placebo effect' validates the reality of the impact of the mind on the body.

"Feelings of anger, apathy, gloom and resentment can weaken the immune system and damage health, whereas positive thoughts of love, compassion, joy, humour and the like support physical health.

"Every thought has a physical effect on your cells. Negative thoughts, particularly about disease and death can literally kill you."

Some men may not handle sickness very well and therefore need to understand the principles of positive thinking. One of them is found in Job 22:28 – "You will also decree a thing, and it will be established for you; and light will shine on your ways".

The decree is made in the thoughts. On the road to health and healing, most damage is not done by the negativity of others but by our own negative internal self-talk – our "mutter chat".

In 2003, I was catapulted into a health journey, commencing with unexplained weight loss. Prayer and seeking God's will launched me onto a platform of positive thinking. My husband, the quintessential optimist, joined me there. Women need such men; men who understand the principles of positive thinking and live by them. Healing begins in the mind.

I thoroughly concur with Raymond Francis' comment from his book *Never Be Sick Again*: "Having a purpose, a higher meaning to your life than mere existence, is a critical part of the whole picture of health." You may call it positive thinking or call it faith.

At times vilified by logical thinkers, faith in a Creator God can generate healing thoughts: "As a man thinketh in his heart, so is he." – Proverbs 23:7.

Positive thinking does not make us immortal but it can contribute to longevity.

Men, think positively! Think life!

Appendix 4

⸻❈⸻

This article is reprinted with the kind permission of the Nation Publishing Co. Limited. It was published in the Weekend Nation on Friday, November 14, 2003.

Special thanks must go to Sonya Jackson who facilitated my writing the article for the Nation Newspaper.

Enjoying Life Her Choice – Divine Inspiration

Contributor: Nola Estwick

Catherine Esther Layne was diagnosed with cancer last October and underwent an operation and chemotherapy treatments – which were initially thought to be successful.

However, the further development of the cancer proved otherwise and a second operation was suggested. Having prayed and weighed the alternatives, Esther decided against it since the operation would leave her somewhat incapacitated.

In the process of her illness, Esther was in and out of hospital. June would see her final admission.

Her condition deteriorated until she finally passed peacefully away on Saturday, July 12, at the Queen Elizabeth Hospital at 7:20 p.m.

Throughout this entire experience as attested by her husband, daughter, other family members and friends, Esther maintained a calm, serene, submissive, peaceful and very dignified demeanour.

According to her husband Tony, she went through the experience "like a trooper." She never once complained, grumbled, fretted, blamed anyone or asked "why me?"

As a devout Seventh-day Adventist, Esther lived her faith. According to her daughter, even when she was in the hospital, she tried to be a s little trouble to the nurses as possible. She was indeed the epitome of what it means to be kept by the power of god, to be held in the hollow of His hand.

Esther bore her pain courageously and possibly she shielded her family from the full extent of her trial. Her calm and resilient spirit was evident to all who visited her.

Her daughter Kathy remembers her as someone who always aimed for excellence, someone who was very organized. She undoubtedly influenced Kathy's vocation as a secretary. Her husband tony remembers her as a loving and forgiving person and she always expected the best of him, she always expected him to do the right thing.

Her son Junior said she always gave him good advice, she never told him anything that was wrong. She was always there for them.

I was indeed blessed to have been able to witness God's power at work in Esther's life as she responded to her illness. When Esther alerted me to the problem, she did so with a request for me to join her in prayer.

We spoke on the phone several times and we prayed together. In all of my contacts with Esther – on the phone, visiting her at home and in the hospital – I realized that she understood one of life's most profound truths. This truth formed the bedrock of her indomitable and lustrous courage.

As she placed her hand trustingly in her Maker's, she understood that ultimately the most important thing was for an individual to desire to fulfill the will of God, indeed to live in His perfect will. She understood the concept of "the bigger picture" and thus her keynote was "whatever is God's will I am content."

The Thursday before her passing I visited her and read to her a letter which I was strongly impressed to write. This letter expressed the sentiments of my heart I believe, as inspired by God, to encourage His child.

Esther was very lucid, wide awake and understood everything I said to her. We were alone as I bent close to her and had full eye contact. She even had occasion to smile once or twice. Following are excerpts from the letter, which I read to her just tow days before her passing.

"Esther, the way you have passed through your trial has been an honour to your God. You have said a lot by your patient and submissive attitude... your faith and love at this trying time have served as a monumental sermon to all of us.

You will be called to sleep for a while, to you it will be the twinkle of an eye, and then you will see your Blessed Redeemer, the One who carried you from your birth and cared for you tenderly in all of life's situations... though physically, you have been getting weaker, yet in spirit, inside of you, God has made something beautiful, something enduring. Continue to hold on firmly to the indisputable fact that nothing can separate us from the love of God. You are loved no less on a bed of affliction than when you were in the days of sunshine. Esther, you have been nothing less than a shining jewel for God.

We all desire to meet you in the morning, it's not goodbye but it's "see you in the morning".

When I left Esther's bedside that Thursday night there was no grief lump, no feeling of depression. There was the wonderful and calm assurance that she was in good hands... she had fought a good fight; she had kept the faith and could say in concert with the apostle Paul, "henceforth is laid up for me a crown of righteousness".

The following quotation was at the end of Esther's letter: "Suffering is a test of faith... if God's love calls you in suffering, respond by self-surrender, and you will learn the mystery of love.

I have dedicated this poem to Esther's memory, originally written for another stalwart of faith who passed away last year. This poem not only epitomizes our memories of Esther but in a sense the essence of her wonderful and indomitable courage will be immortalised in our hearts through its words. She was indeed "a shining jewel for God.

A Beautiful Life...

Is like a piece of tapestry into which God has blended
And interwoven the colourful qualities of His own nature...
Gentleness, kindness, compassion and deep caring
Producing a canvas on which the master Artist
Has inscribed His signature.
A beautiful life pulsates and radiates with
The tenderness of God.
Like the calm in the eye of a storm...
It knows that peace which passeth all understanding
In the midst of trial and perplexity calmly acknowledging
That God is a fortress wherein lies safety.
Touching, loving, healing, forgiving, nurturing and
Selflessly giving until there is no more left...

And such a life she lived...
A wonderfully sweet wife, mother, grandmother,
Sister, friend and confidant.
She lived a life of hope and nurtured hope in others.
The lustre of her life shines beyond the grave
In the lives it has illuminated... even for a brief time.
A beautiful life never dies
For its memories are indelibly etched in the
minds of those it has succoured.
Our loved one, though departed, has left us
A treasure of inestimable price
May she rest in peace until that great morning.

Published Weekend Nation Friday, November 14, 2003

Appendix 5

Special Edition - October 2005

Theme: Women Mentoring Women

My Dear Friends,

What an awesome God we serve! I received such an exquisitely delightful piece of correspondence from one of my Adventure Prayer Team Trench Warriors.

Of course she would want to remain anonymous. I do think she will recognize herself as she reads and will no doubt smile and wonder what I will get up to next.

I will call my friend, let's see, 'June', is a good enough pseudonym.

I am always blessed, refreshed and encouraged whenever June writes to me. I told her that I was so thrilled with her letter that I would have to respond with another letter. The letter is all the more special because she delivered it by hand to my work place. And, that was not the first occasion!

I want to respond to June's letter and I have been prompted to invite you to 'eavesdrop' as I share my heart with June. In fact, you do not even need to eavesdrop! Come and take a ring side seat as I share June's insights with me and reciprocate with mine. This is a learning experience for all of us.

June is not just praying for me, but she is truly interceding. I discovered in my reading that there is a difference. She tells me that she prays for me every morning and evening. With her consistent coverage, your prayers too, plus mine, I think God must already have said to one of His angels: 'Let them know the deed is done, they can keep praying but turn the prayers into praises. All will be well. I can never retract Numbers 23:19. My character is staked on that! '

So take your seat, while I chat with June. I will draw you into the "conversation" as I deem necessary.

My Dear June,

Now it is time for our tete a tete! I hope you do not mind me inviting the others along. Since you are invisible, your anonymity is safe!

You have always been a very positive inspiration to me. This is not just now, but it goes years back. What you have been sharing with me in the valley is quite inspiring. It seems as though you have the knack for saying the right thing at the right time. God sends you along to back up something He has told me. Of course we both know about "Divine orchestration".

Well, as I told you on the phone, I decided to wait until I reached home to savor my letter. What you said on the outside of the envelope captured my attention and may I add emotions. In the staff room was not the place to read your letter.

Team, this was what June had written on the envelope:

"There is not one drop of wrath in the cup you are drinking

He took all that was bitter out of it, and left it a cup of love."

Extracted from 'Words of Comfort and Cheer'

by Mrs. Charles Cowman October 24, pg 282

June, I love that quote and understand that you understand!!!! Actually, it reminded me of a statement from one of my favourite books 'The Ministry of Healing'. A very similar sentiment is expressed in the following:

"In every trial if we seek Him, Christ will give us help. Our eyes will be opened to discern the healing promises recorded in His word. The Holy Spirit will teach us how to appropriate every blessing that will be an antidote to grief. For every bitter draft that is placed to our lips, we shall find a branch of healing." Pg 248

I know beyond the shadow of any doubt that the purpose of my loving Heavenly Father is to refine me. Even in that process He has been so very gentle. He knows how to regulate the process. Though there may be occasions when tears flow because we are human, His sweet encouraging presence in our hearts can turn tears of sadness into tears of joy because we know, we have that confidence, that He IS working all things out for our best good.

Malachi 3:14 says: He shall sit as a refiner and purifier of silver and He shall purify the sons of Levi and purge them as gold and silver, that they may offer unto the Lord an offering in righteousness.

So once we understand that it is really about purging and refining and purifying, then we can submit and not fight God. The word 'sit' is to be noted. God never leaves the process unattended. He sits there and regulates the heat of the furnace. God and God alone knows when it would be safe to turn the heat off.

I have told God that when it is over that I do not want to come out as 'fool's gold'. I do not want to be half baked! I will endure the process to the end because I want the very best God has for me! Is it ever really all over though? Not really, the process will end when Christ comes!!

Jesus endured right through to the very end for me. I have accepted His call on my heart to take up my cross and follow Him.

June, you know that we glibly sing, many songs without considering the depth of the lyrics and what they really signify! Let us consider the words of this beautiful song. The last time I sang it at a church; I smiled as I asked myself if as a congregation we really meant the level of commitment we were singing:

I will follow thee my Saviour whereso'er my lot may be
Where thou goest I will follow; yes my Lord I will follow thee.
Though the road be rough and thorny, trackless as the foaming sea
Thou hast trod this way before me, And I'll **gladly** follow thee.

Yes, as disciples, we are called to follow our Master. It is not a reluctant, halfhearted, resigned kind of following. No! The love of God in our hearts must be the fuel to allow us to follow and fall into line with the plans God has for us.......good plans!!!

I love the second paragraph of your letter and I agree with you 100%! Team, this is what June said:

"I like how God sends encouragement through thoughts that renew our faith as we wait for the outworking of His providences. These insights maintain our communication, remind us that our relationship with Him is real, confirm what He has said, and assure us that our wait won't be in vain. Before an insight gets overworked, God renews us with another and another. And the multiplied evidence heightens our faith".

Team, you would realize that June is quite articulate. She really does hit the nail on the head with that nice bit of well-crafted eloquence. I have told June that she can write a book.

June, how very correct you are. God really does corroborate and confirm and affirm. In fact at one of the churches I spoke, I told the congregation that I would have to be dumb, deaf, blind and mentally challenged not to hear God and see His leading. Right now with all the accumulated evidence it is much easier to believe than to doubt.

Reflections on Valley Experiences

You reminded me of a thought you shared earlier where you quoted from 'Candles in the Dark'. The writer said: "We are never staying in the valley or rough waters. We are always only passing through them. We get through our valley times leaning on "Our Beloved".

The metaphor of the valley is thick with lessons. Psalm 84 speaks of the 'Valley of Baca' which means the valley of weeping. Yet, it is also a valley of springs and replenishment. Interestingly enough when you gave me the letter, I also handed you prayer letter 17 which spoke about the desert and valley places being the very places where the most Heavenly treasure can be garnered.

Did you realize that we exchanged some of the same very insights but they were just couched in different language? Now we both know that it is not coincidental. It speaks to the kind of repackaging of insights you alluded to which God does time and again so we can get the message more clearly. You reminded me that God would support me and bring me out triumphantly.

It seems as though you have the scoop on how God works because your words of wisdom are dead on. Now I know you did not look into a crystal ball to make that kind of proleptic comment.

Team, this is what my insightful friend said: "As the divine Physician of both body and soul He knows how to adjust your physical machinery to bring about your recovery."

June must have been attending classes held by this same Great Physician. She has confirmed exactly what God told me from the very beginning. God made my body and if anything goes wrong with it, He knows exactly how it should be fixed. He made it and has the master key!!!

What I love about God is that He is not into "tinkering and practising". He is not playing any guessing game. 'Oh, let's see now' what is wrong? Well, it could be one of three things! '

(Excuse the Bajan parlance) Next ting ya know I cock up and dead and it en even from one a de tree tings!!!!" I must admit at such a time as this I would rather fall into the hands of God than the hands of man.

Team, my friend listened to a sermon entitled "The Fourth Man" and she found it very inspirational as it was in fact the answer to a prayer request. She extracted five principles which she said captured her mind.

So let me get back to my chat with June as I share with you what she took the time to share with me. Talk about mentoring!!!! Go girl!!!!

These principles are couched in her own expression as she has read and synthesized for me. By the way, June is a bright spark. She would never admit it though.

Principle #1: "True faith will be tried- there will be a place, a time, a situation in your life and mine when we will be tried, when the faith we have in God, the songs we sing about His reality,

284

the declaration of our faith and our love and our commitment to Him will be tested."

Well, June you know that this is my time and you had and are still having yours. The truth of the matter is that it is the storm that tests the worth of the ship. The storm reveals whether we really trust God or not.

June, you remember Prayer Letter # 7 with the health scare? The sky was only set up then and I was consumed with fear. Thank God that my weakness was revealed before the clouds burst.

I found this very interesting quote from another of my favourite books: *Christ' Object Lessons*. Inspiration says:

"It is in a crisis that character is revealed. ...A sudden and unlooked for calamity, something that brings the soul face to face with death, will show whether there is any rea faith in the promises of God". Pg 326 Quite a poignant statement!

The second principle you shared had to do with compromise. "You will encounter the choice of faith versus compromise every day of your life, everywhere you will be called to exercise your faith in God or some aspect of Christian living. The devil is after you, **but the power of God is overshadowing you.** God is calling out to you – Hold on to your faith. Don't compromise."

June, the part you placed in bold called to memory a dream that a friend had about me. She told me that she dreamt that we were in a house, and we were talking about the Lord. She looked outside and saw on a hill top a number of persons dressed in black rowed off in a line. They had their hands shading their eyes looking in the direction of the house. She was led to believe that they were looking for me, but I was safely under the covering of the house.

From that dream my friend told me that she understood that the enemy was out for my life but I was protected by God. This is the same friend who gave me a letter in 'uncanny' circumstances telling me that I would live and not die.

I know that I am under the shadow of His wings. There I am safely abiding until the storm passes. Under His wings is a source of great strength and that is why I can keep up with all this writing and all the other things I am doing!

I love your words of confidence and instruction: ….if you hold on to your faith, God will see to it that if you don't bow you won't burn. Something miraculous will happen to deliver you because your faith is your victory. When you live by faith you are on the winning side."

June, I appreciate tremendously that you were not only edified by what you read but you saw its relevance to me and took time to share it. I believe that the miracle is already happening but because it is slow and continuous it does not seem dramatic and well, let's say cataclysmic.

A dramatic end to this health scenario would be for me to go into a crisis type situation where it became obvious that if God did not intervene I would clearly die. God then swoops down and snatches me from the jaws of death. We are all left with our mouths agape.

I must say that that sounds adventurous, exciting, thrilling and would be a nail biting finish to what seems a rather drawn out….. no, not ordeal!! Definitely not!!! Let's say, extended journey, because it is really that. It is a journey toward God and a journey into myself and what I really think and believe about God at the very deepest level.

God has confirmed to my heart time and again not to be concerned so much with the length of the journey but I should enjoy the scenery as I travel and learn well all of the lessons along the way.

I do have a sense that this is a slow cooker miracle. While I may 'metaphorise' the process, I have evidence that some positive changes are transpiring in my body. I still have evidences of the process of degeneration, a process I believe that has started to reverse since without surgery and any kind of drugs I have gained weight. It is to keep gaining and in the correct places too!!!

I do not gauge God's work by how I feel, I gauge His work based on His word, what He said. So even if it looked as if there was no progress, I would see progress with the eye of faith. But in my spirit, in the inner man, or more specifically woman, I have remained elated, bubbly, optimistic, excited and joyous. If positive feelings alone could put your body back in shape, I would be signing up for the next marathon..... and winning it too!

For me, this is the most exciting part of the miracle- the emotional stamina God has given to me. I have never been depressed and wondered what would become of me. Those who are mere spectators to my experience must wonder how I am making it. Psalm 71:7 God drew to my attention and we had a little chuckle together.

June, let me take you behind the scenes for a bit. There are times I have felt tired with keeping up with all the things I am doing. But do you know what I absolutely love about God? It is that He does not expect the impossible from us. He is aware that physically and even emotionally at times our strength may sag. And He is always there to replenish. My strength sagging does not for me, mean a sagging of faith. No!!

But I have been and am still going quite a bit: keeping up with the house work, all my school work, my duties at church, attendance at the midweek meetings, my appointments at other churches and preparing the power point presentations for those appointments, juicing, which takes time, going to the gym at 5:00 nearly every morning and of course still spending my quiet time with God. Of course there are also my motherly and wifely duties to keep up with as well. It is obvious to me; if to no one else, God has to be carrying me.

He has just been so awesome in pouring His strength into me. I do recollect one Sunday, I just felt as though I was on a treadmill. I am often at the sink washing wares. I do get help but it seems washing dishes is a never ending job, because there is always cooking and eating. I think the energy and time that a woman gives of herself in the kitchen is often underestimated. I can see many heads nodding!!

Anyhow, as I stood by the sink after lunch, such a feeling of weariness came over me, as well as some feelings of resentment, I must admit. I felt that I always seemed to be the one at it all the time. I do most of the juicing myself, Andy would help at times, more so early up, when I was at it twice a day and juicing quite a lot of vegetables. No one can go to the gym for me; I have to do that myself.

Well, I reflected on the length of time I had been traveling and how much longer I would have to go on with this routine. The tears just started to flow. At the same time I heard a knocking and I hastily wiped my eyes. I learnt that you were out there, June. I could not let you know I was in a bit of a bad mood.

I went out to meet you at your car and you gave me a letter. We chatted a bit and then you left. It was clear that your visit there and then was not a coincidence. Well, I left the dishes and went and sat in the hammock and read your letter.

It was an "oasis time".

Oh boy!!! There it was, you spoke about God responding to our unspoken thoughts and in your letter to me He was doing just that!!! Well, it was a mixture of laughing and crying but my spirits were instantly lifted!!! I went back and finished the dishes pondering on the ways of this God we serve.

Those who do not know Him and how He comes right on time to meet our needs are missing, not half, but all of their lives!!!

Okay, I think I need to get back to filling in the others on the other principles you shared with me.

In Principle #3 you said, "You are freer in the furnace than you are outside – you are freer when you live by faith than when you compromise."

I was invited to share my testimony at one of our churches in Miami and my theme was about being in the furnace. I spoke about that in an earlier letter, if you would recollect.

Yes June, I agree with you. It is the most amazing and fascinating thing to be in a "furnace type" situation and to be perfectly cool- no pretense, no faking, and no dissembling. One can fake happiness more easily that one can fake being at peace, especially over a prolonged period of time. There is a very clear distinction between the peace the world gives and the peace which is from God.

In Principle # 4 you reminded me that when I "stand for God rather than bow down, the Fourth man will stand with me and there is no God who can deliver after this sort!!!

Team, when June refers to the Fourth man she alludes to the story of the three Hebrew boys who were thrown into the furnace because they refused to compromise. Oh, you know about it all already?! But maybe someone who will read this letter later may not be familiar with the story. It is found in the book of Daniel.

The final principle # 5: You said "You are going to win because the Fourth man goes into the fiery furnace with you, robs the fire of its violence and brings you out unharmed. June, those very powerful words are not only for me, but will bring strength and courage to the heart of some person who will be called to a fiery experience sometime in the future.

The metaphorical language of the "fire being robbed of its violence" is so very true in my experience. I can still see my ribs and skeletal frame but I see way past the bones and see what an ingenious God I serve who knows how to orchestrate a master plan for my life.

Yes, I totally agree when you say: "I love serving a God like that! He is worthy of our trust". Absolutely!!

June, you are one person who has bought right into my metaphor of "The Adventure Prayer Team". You have signed several of your correspondences to me using that appellation! I know that you are totally in sync with me and do not consider me "strange" as some may possibly have, who only got to letter Prayer Letter No 3 or so.

Possibly some may have said: 'What madness is this? She is defying the doctor's orders and playing with her health. Some people take this religion thing too far!!!'.

Well, June, I have kept you long but you seem to avidly dig into these letters. I thought I wanted to let you know and the others who are traveling with me, how much I appreciate your warm and palpable support. I think of myself as an athlete running around a track, sprinting to win a race. Only this time my track is the track of life. I know I have quite a few spectators; some are far away in the stands and look on wondering if I will make it.

The thing about spectators is that once the athlete gets far along the track away from the crowd, he can no longer hear the cheering. I have been at the stadium where I have seen someone leave his position of "spectatorism" and begin to run on the grass next to the runner. He is there to shout words of encouragement to him and to keep pace with him as he makes his way to the finish line.

Such support can never be given from the stands and it takes someone with spiritual stamina to undertake to run next to the runner, especially when it is a race of marathon proportions. June, I know for sure that you and others are on the track with me. You are breathing with me and keeping pace with me. Real deep intercessory prayer is like running on the grass next to someone.

There are some of you I do not see often because of our schedules. Some of my friends are overseas. But I know who my runners are and let me thank all of you for your prayer support. You have been standing in the gap for me. You have been claiming Heaven's power for me to keep going.

Your prayers have not been in vain. Not at all!!! We are yet to understand the potency of prayer. To live in the will of God we must pray in the will of God. You have been running this race vicariously with me. But Jesus has done what no other human being can do for me. He stepped into my human shoes over 2000 years ago and has assured me that because He lives I will live too. Now, and eternally!

I know that I have Him as the Fourth man in the furnace with me and it is He who has been constantly renewing my strength, every single day.

Well, I will continue to tear down the track. Some of my runners may need to stop and rest at times, but I will pick you back up when I am making another lap.

As we are all called to run our own race, Hebrews 12:1 tells us: Wherefore seeing we are encompassed about with so great a cloud of witnesses .....let us run with patience the race that is set before us.

Victory is assured because Jesus Himself is the author and finisher of our faith!!

June, thank you for sharing so poignantly with me. Your words will have a ripple effect I am quite sure! You too are a "Daughter of God". You have truly set the example of how women can encourage other women in their valley times. I certainly hope that men have the same kind of set up that we have created. The race continues and I am not yet out of breath! Pun intended!

June, continue to share, your timely words of wisdom and advice will help not only me but all who may someday read this letter.

God Bless You Much!

With Love and Abundant Appreciation,

Nola

About The Author

Nola Estwick is a Barbadian and has been an English teacher for the past thirty five years at the Christ Church Foundation School. She possesses a Bachelor of Arts Degree in English and a Diploma in Education with a Distinction in Teaching Practice. She is married and has three daughters.

Lean on, trust in, *and* be confident in the Lord with all your heart *and* mind and do not rely on your own insight *or* understanding.

In all your ways know, recognize, *and* acknowledge Him, and He will direct and make straight and plain your paths. Proverbs 3: 5 & 6 Amplified Bible